TITANIC THREADS

My thread is cut,
and yet it is not spun,
And now I live,
and now my life is done.

Chidiock Tichborne
(Born Southampton, ca 1558 – died London 1586)
Tichborne's Elegy

MARY L. SOUTH

with Foreword by
TOM BEAUMONT JAMES

HAMAMELIS BOOKS
88, Hamilton Road
Bishopstoke
Eastleigh
SO50 6AN

ISBN 978 0 9571895 0 8

Artwork and layout by The Freelance Design Partnership Ltd.
Malt House Studios, 4 Brook Street, Bishops Waltham, Southampton, Hampshire SO32 1AX

Printed by Imagewise Reprographics Ltd
Unit 5, Parham Drive Boyatt Wood, Eastleigh, Hampshire SO50 4NU.

TITANIC
THREADS

CONTENTS

ACKNOWLEDGEMENTS

The number of people linked to the *Titanic* grows every year. Future descendants of families directly linked to the ship will extend around the globe, with perhaps only vague memories of their attachment, to the disaster. This would have been the fate of the Simmons and James families except that our forebears kept documents; letters, diaries, photographs and postcards, to form our two family archives.

So it is to my late father, Ted Simmons, that I owe the greatest debt, for keeping and cherishing the archive of papers which form the central part of this story and which introduced me to my grandfather, Fred Simmons. Tom James's generous loan of his father's diaries added the all-important extra dimension to the story's concept. I am truly grateful to him for that.

John Nicholas, as the Lucraft family historian, provided me with much of that early history, while Janine Alidjan filled in many of the gaps in the Simmonses background. The late Dorothy Salmon's encyclopaedic memory and her brother, John Baker, added information from their mother's reminiscences about her early life in Southampton. All of these were not only invaluable in building the background to the lives of Fred and Winifred, but also the period in which they lived. I am indebted to them all for reading the initial script and correcting my many errors. Many other family members and friends have provided their support and therefore, added their own threads to the story. I am grateful to every one of them.

The staff at the Southampton City Archives were helpful and patient, despite my many requests and frequent idiosyncrasies. Rachel Wragg, previously from Heritage Services, shared her wealth of *Titanic* knowledge with me, ensuring I did not fall foul of the many myths surrounding the ship. Captain Terry Lilley provided me with information about the shipboard internal monetary system and John Markham, in Australia, explained the significance of the uniform buttons.

Despite so much help and support there will be errors which remain, these are my responsibility alone.

MLS
2011

FOREWORD

This charming and moving little book draws together previously unpublished fragments of family archives and sets them in the context of some major events: the loss of the *Titanic* in 1912 and the First and Second World Wars together with a meticulously researched family history. It provides new perspectives on an apparently well-known event, casting significant new light in particular on the *Titanic* disaster and the aftermath in Southampton. As the book shows, it was entirely fortuitous that the author and I discovered we had a shared connection through Southampton with the *Titanic* disaster and also that her family and mine had been involved together in more than one tragic event in Southampton's twentieth century history. But there were happy times as well with children of both families growing up in the Blighmont area in the Millbrook parish of the town and the marriage of Fred Simmons's widow at Holy Trinity Millbrook being the first such ceremony conducted by my father as the new Rector of the parish in 1917. Nor did the crossing of family paths end there as the story shows...

One of the curiosities that this interesting tale reveals is that one of the children of a *Titanic* victim was named 'Ernest Hope' at baptism by my father. This by coincidence was the name which my grandfather, Charles Thomas Clement James (1859-1930) had chosen for himself in his semi-autobiographical and rather naughty three-decker novel *Always Wrong* published in 1895. I wonder what father was thinking as he baptised that child in the sad aftermath of the loss of the *Titanic*?

TBJ

12.2011

INTRODUCTION

Woman: I see you contributed to *Titanic Voices*.

Man: Did I? What's *Titanic Voices*?

Woman: A book produced from recollections about how the disaster affected the families of the crew and Southampton people in general. It was published in 1994.

Man: Well, my father as a young clergyman had to break bad news to some of his parishioners who had lost family on the ship.

Woman: You *are* the right Tom James – that's the story in the book.

Man: So what's your connection to *Titanic*, Mary?

Woman: My father, Ted Simmons, was one of the contributors to the book. He was raised on the Titanic Fund. His father, Fred Simmons, was one of the stewards and drowned in the wreck.

Further discussion revealed curious coincidences in the two family histories. For a large part of the intervening years between the First World War and the Second World War they had lived in close proximity along Regent's Park Road, in the Southampton parish of Millbrook. One of the Simmons family lived at the top end of the road, Winifred, my grandmother, and her Simmons/Baker family lived next door to the Post Office, about halfway down the road and the Reverend James Lyne Beaumont James, Tom's father, known to his friends as Beau, lived at the Rectory with his family in the 1930s, midway between the two Simmons family groups. Members of the families would have met occasionally and no doubt knew one another by sight. Tom James's brothers had been born at the Blighmont Nursing Home, adjacent to Regent's Park Road between 1925 and 1940, and Tom was born there after the war. Outside, in the Blighmont grounds, I spent large amounts of my childhood in the old walled garden, discovering birds' nests and learning the rudiments of horticulture. Mr Pointer, our neighbour, was the gardener there and kept the Nursing Home supplied with fresh vegetables for the kitchen and cut flowers for the wards; he also makes appearances in James's detailed diaries of those days. Against the outside wall of the garden were two pigsties and a chicken run. These provided home grown pork, chicken meat and fresh eggs, for the patients. The front lawn of the Nursing Home was kept 'out of bounds' by six patrolling 'guard geese', who took their duties very seriously. Only the crisp crackle of Matron's starched apron, as she bustled across the lawn, could be guaranteed to scatter them in fear.

Despite our different backgrounds, the *Titanic* disaster had been a focal point in both our family histories, with the memory remaining throughout the subsequent generations. The differences in our backgrounds however, serve not only to illustrate the influence of the disaster on our own family members at the time, but also how the communities within the town of Southampton coped with the disaster. The ship touched many lives, none more so than here, where most of the crew had lived. Out of eight hundred and ninety-eight crew, more than five hundred came from the Southampton area.

During its long history as a significant port, dating from the medieval period to the present time, the town had become familiar with shipping accidents, but usually these were linked with trading or military operations. Towards the end of the nineteenth century however, there began a subtle shift, from its role as an import and export centre, to one linked with foreign travel particularly to and from the Americas. Sailing ships had almost disappeared with the advent of the steamships, which had used both steam and sail. The age of the great liners had begun and these carried wealthy people in comfortable cabins and others, often emigrants, in more basic 'steerage' accommodation. Further progress with engine development meant that by the end of the century even the steamships were becoming obsolete. Powerful engines led to bigger boats and the ability to carry more passengers. Even the local 'Yacht Laundry' at Millbrook reflected the change and by the mid-1920s had become 'Liners Laundry'.

In 1907 Southampton welcomed White Star Line, the most prestigious of the passenger carriers. By promising to build a larger dock for the Company's liners, the port had wooed White Star away from Liverpool.[1] Now the most important of the Company's ships would operate from Southampton. The arrival of the first White Star liner, the *Adriatic*, caused the Mayor and Corporation to commission one of the local paddle steamers; then, with all the flags flying in celebration of the occasion, they steamed out to meet the *Adriatic* and accompany her to the newly built White Star Dock, later to become the Ocean Dock.

The town was booming and people in search of work flocked into the neighbourhood. The opportunities to outsiders seemed endless with the expansion of the docks; there was building work needing labour, manpower was needed for the docks and dockside industries, the associated railway, the ships needed crew, hotels needed more staff and the town's expanding population needed services as well. There seemed to be something for everyone and Southampton became a magnet, for both skilled and unskilled individuals, seeking work.

Conditions in some areas of the town were not good, with over-crowded houses accommodating large families and even more over-crowded lodging houses, for those hoping for employment. A popular local tradition stated that lodging houses offered a shared bed for threepence (1.5p) a night for each occupant of the bed, or men could sleep 'on the line' for one penny (0.4p). 'The lines' were supposedly strung across the dormitories and the lodgers hung their arms over this, with their heads either hanging over the line as well, or resting on one shoulder. Arranged like this they attempted to get some rest before returning either to some place of work, or to the various labour hiring agencies in the town. The sharing of beds was common (see Appendix 1, cycle ride account) and the records show this was the case in the lodging houses, although the story of 'the line' may be apocryphal. At sea the sharing of bunks and hammocks was not unusual, as one man woke and went on shift, so his returning comrade took his place in the bunk or hammock – a system known as 'hot-bedding'.

At the turn of the twentieth century, some areas of the town were due for clearance, having been condemned as unfit for human habitation in the mid-nineteenth century. Fashionable visitors had been complaining about the conditions in some areas of the town since the early nineteenth century. One described the area formerly occupied by the medieval royal castle, but at that time surrounding the Marquis of Lansdowne's unfinished gothic castle, on the same site, as 'situated in the worst part of the Town, very confined and surrounded with mean little hovels occupied by the lowest description of poor people'.[2] Ninety years later, for some inhabitants in the small airless courts near St Michael's church and around the Docks, living conditions were still the same.[3] For others living along the River Itchen, to the east of the town, being closer to the Docks meant being closer to the main industrial developments of the town, wood yards, gasworks, sawmills, and the coal wharves were just a few of the industries established there, with their attendant environmental health hazards of dust and fumes. Nonetheless these too offered employment opportunities for incomers.

Despite all the advances in marine engine technology, which resulted in the increased size of shipping, the Board of Trade lagged far behind in its safety regulations for the large passenger vessels of the early twentieth century and shipping companies were not inclined to upgrade their own requirements in isolation. As a result, the large liners steamed across the Atlantic equipped with hopelessly inadequate numbers of lifeboats for all those on board, if an emergency should arise. The *Titanic* disaster proved the point only too well and nowhere was it more keenly felt than in Southampton.

It is apparent that the lives of the immediate families connected with the disaster would be directly affected by the death, in many cases, of the main breadwinner. But the effects were felt not only by the close family; the repercussions spread out into the previous generation and would be felt by the next, perhaps even the third generation. This became apparent through the Simmons archive and explained the traditional Simmons/Baker Christmas toast to the *Titanic*. The reason behind such an apparently macabre tradition is not immediately apparent, but if the *Titanic* disaster had not happened, none of the family members making the toast, would have been born. Without the death of her first husband on the ship, Winifred Simmons would not have been free to marry Robert Baker, with the resulting birth of their four children. Similarly her first child Edward Simmons, my father, would not have been raised and apprenticed at the expense of the Titanic Fund, with the result that with the skills

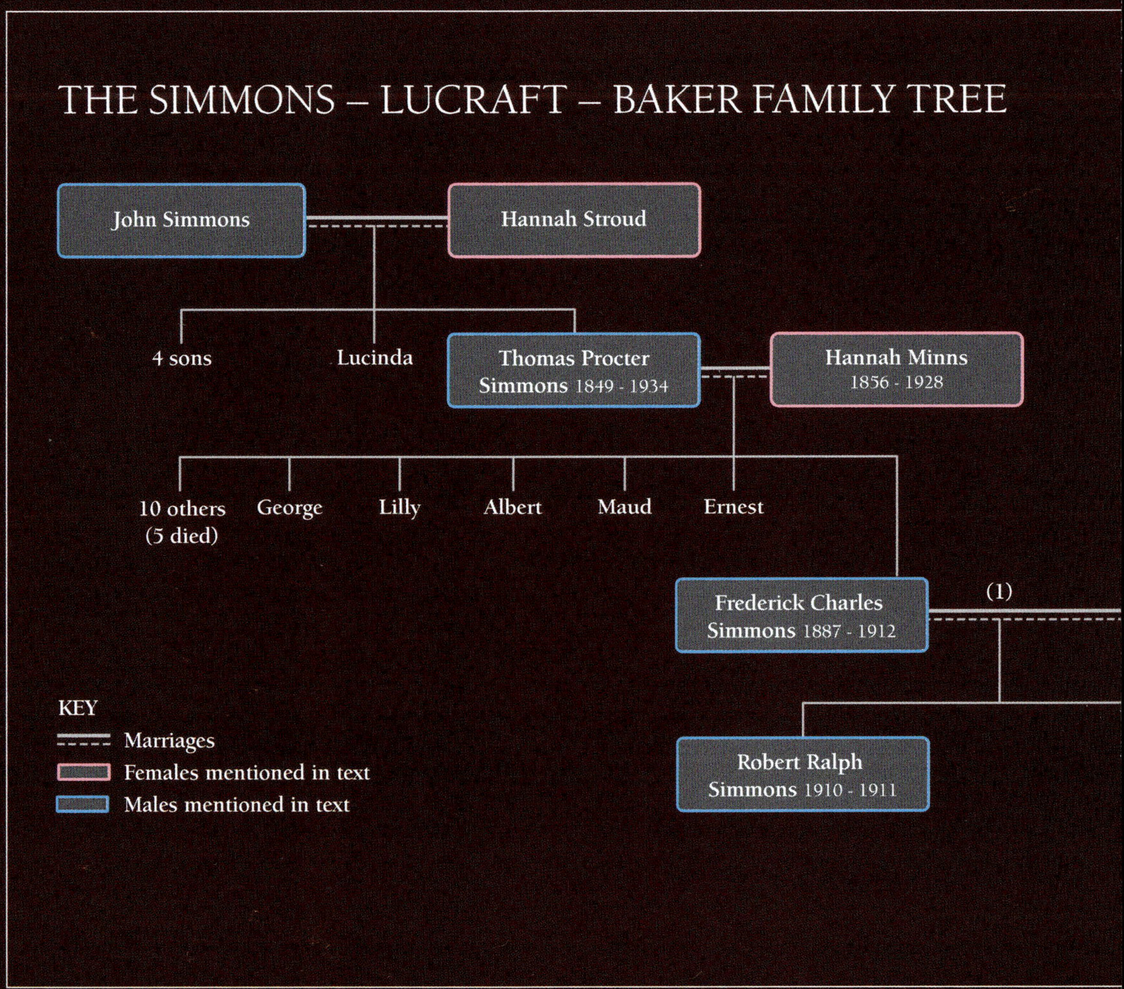

he learnt, he was able to move to Bristol, in 1933, for a better job opportunity. There he met and married my mother, Lily, before they returned to Southampton four years later. Without that meeting in Bristol, I would not be writing this book. Events following the disaster had rewritten the expected family history and none of Winifred's four Baker children, nor any of her grandchildren, would have been born without the loss of the *Titanic*.

It was not only the families of the crew who were affected, however; others were drawn into the drama and they became threads in the tapestry as well. The White Star Line staff

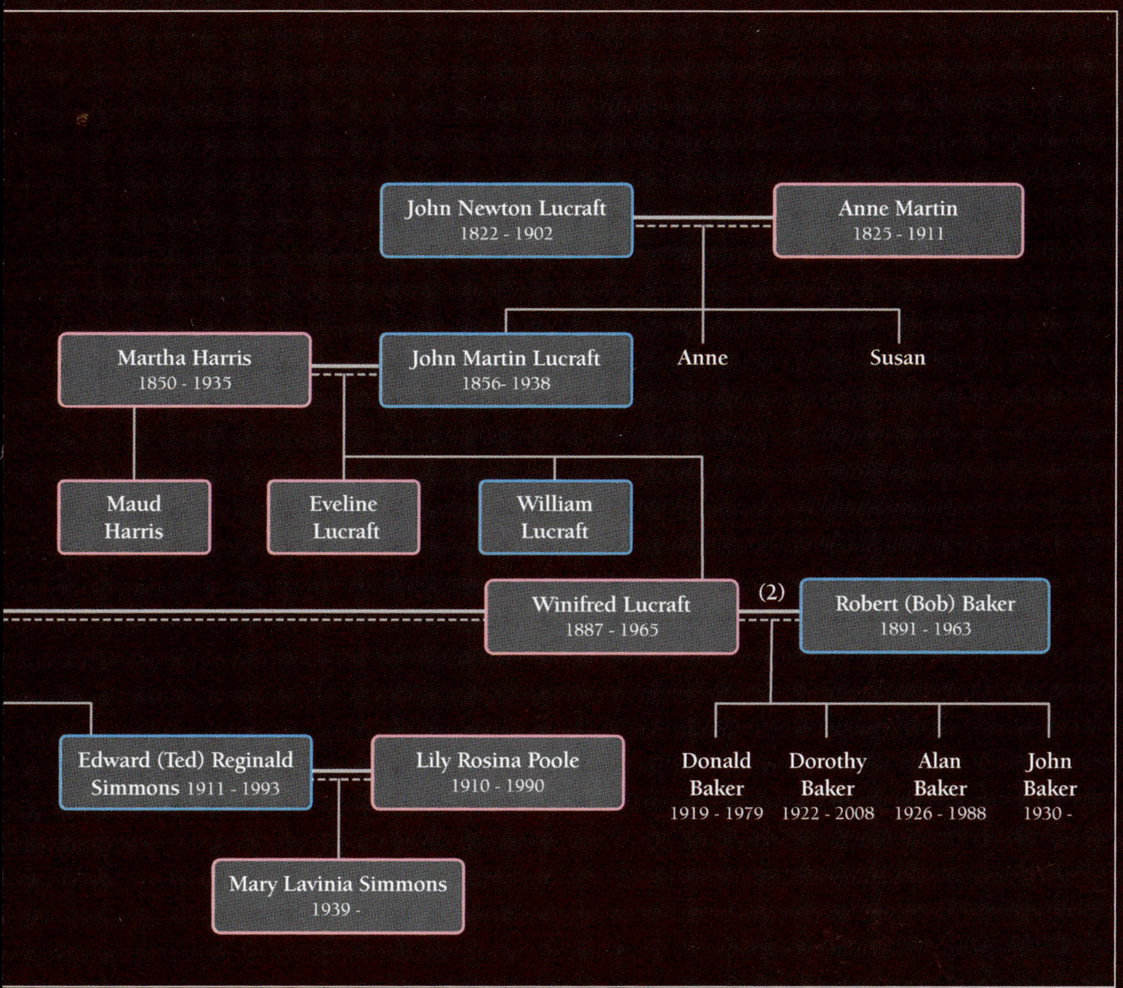

never expected to have to deal with such a calamity; their agent in the far off backwater of Halifax, in Nova Scotia, never expected to find himself coping with the recovery and burial of large numbers of bodies; and a newly appointed young curate, in a Southampton parish, never expected to find himself facing a large number of grieving and anguished families, just over a year after his ordination.

Using the Simmons family archive as the main thread for the story, it progresses from the late nineteenth century up until the 1920s, and briefly looks at some of the social attitudes of the period and various experiences of the family members. Why did an apparently prosperous working class family from a small Devonshire village become linked with a family of Southampton dock workers? What were living conditions and schools like for them? And what series of events brought them into close proximity to the Reverend Beaumont James?

The map covers the areas of the town most closely linked to the various sections and periods of the story, showing their relationship to one another. From this it is possible to appreciate how the family fortunes gradually improved over the years, moving from the unpleasant surroundings alongside the River Itchen and Docks, to the more congenial regions of Millbrook and Shirley. Both these last areas were still relatively rural until the 1950s, when large scale rehousing development took place in response to the needs created by the damage of the Second World War. Although undated, there are various inaccuracies in the map which suggest a date in the early 1930s for its original production.

Because the text draws on personal archive material large sections in some chapters are based on the writings, tape recordings and personal reminiscences of various people. Thus, there are fragments of conversation recorded, as handed down in the oral tradition, and quotations from letters and diaries are included. Other background material from other sources has been inserted, either to clarify or extend the context when necessary and there has been some attempt to maintain the 'voices' of the original 'contributors'. Where specific points of historical accuracy have been raised these are included in the endnotes, as are some of the words and colloquialisms favoured by my grandfather, Fred, in his writing. Wherever facts directly pertaining to the *Titanic* itself, as in the 'Titanic' chapter, have been used, these have been drawn directly from John Eaton and Charles Haas's classic reference book *Titanic – Triumph and Tragedy*. Its encyclopaedic knowledge of minutiae made it, together with the Southampton oral history book, *Titanic Voices*, invaluable for this undertaking. However, the many references and resulting endnotes to either publication would be tedious within the text, so these have not been included. My apologies for any difficulty this decision may cause the reader. Of necessity, there are sections of the story that have required some speculation;

Southampton road map circa 1930

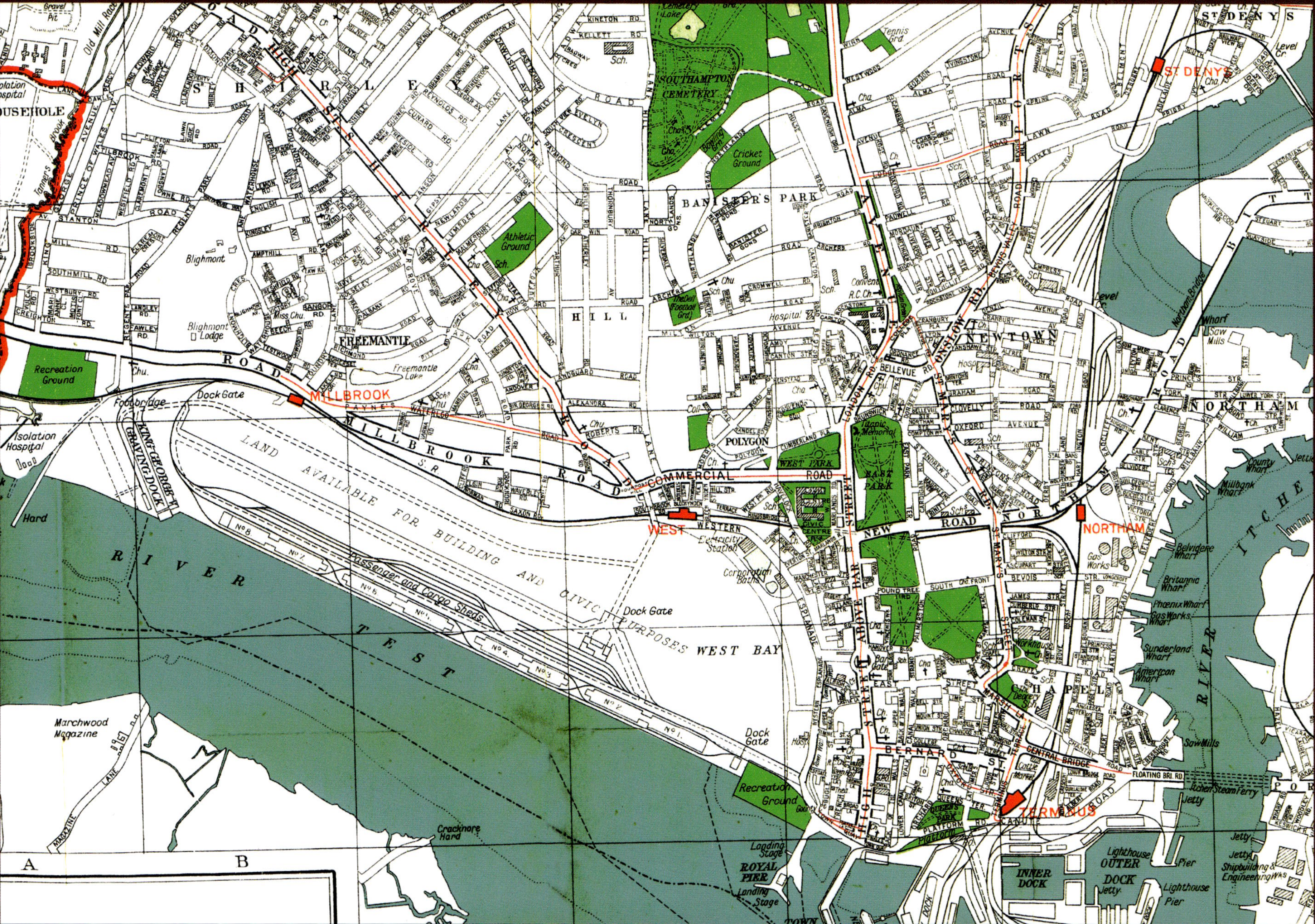

these are not intended to mislead or detract from the main narrative facts, but rather to carry the story forward and illustrate it more clearly.

The *Frontispiece* painting perhaps reflects more clearly than anything else the extending thread of the disaster through the family generations. After reading the initial text draft, Winifred and Fred's great grandson, Keith South, felt the need, after fifteen years away from his paintbrushes, to produce a painting of the ship – in his own idiosyncratic way. The title 'Painting 401', means exactly that – before she was launched, *Titanic* was known only by her Belfast hull construction number, 401, and the picture shows it being painted.

During the writing of this piece, it has not been the intention to allocate blame, pass judgements or make criticisms of any organisation or individual, but only to record the events as they seem to have affected the central groups. People's reactions are placed, as far as possible, within the context of their own social standing, in an attempt to illustrate how they coped with the tragedy, not to discriminate against their actions. Any attempt to pass judgement should be seen as futile, present day values and attitudes can never be applied successfully to past events, unless the same attitudes were in effect within the earlier society.

Piecing the stories together has been a long and sometimes painful process, but my abiding feeling now, is one of utmost regard for the women of that era. Although they were still regarded as subordinate to their men folk, their strength of character and fortitude when coping with the circumstances which overtook them, should earn our highest respect.

MLS
2011

CHAPTER 1

BEGINNINGS

They stood together, a small group of people, a young couple, their parents and a few friends in Southampton High Street. Number 23 looked more like an estate agent's office than the Registrar, but the plaque outside clearly proclaimed that this was the Registrar's Office, licensed for marriages. They went in and were ushered through to an office at the back.

Standing in front of Mr Hunt the Registrar, the girl looked down at the floor and the young man nervously twisted the cap in his hands.

"Thomas Procter Simmons?" asked the Registrar.

"Yes, sir," came the reply.

"And you are twenty-one?"

"Yes, sir, that's right."

"And you, young lady are Hannah Minns?"

"Yes, sir," scarcely above a whisper.

"And your age?"

"Nineteen, sir."

"So you are not yet of age?"

"No, sir."

"Who gives permission for this girl to be wed?"

"I do, sir. I am her father and may I be so bold as to say that she is known as Annie, sir."

"Very well. I shall proceed."

A few minutes later on 27 April 1873, they left the office as Mr and Mrs Thomas Simmons. It was not an auspicious start to their marriage, but not an unusual one either. Annie was pregnant and so the arrangements had been made in some haste. Whether haste or embarrassment was the cause of their confusion, both of them had given inaccurate information about their ages. Thomas was twenty-four years old not twenty-one; there was however, some excuse for his mistake - he had been three years old before he was baptised, so may have calculated his birthday from then. Annie was seventeen years old; the reason for her misinformation is easy to understand – 'aged nineteen' sounded slightly more responsible, than being aged seventeen, when undertaking a marriage contract and motherhood.

Thomas's father John Simmons, had died nine years earlier, when Thomas was fifteen. As a result the family had had to leave their pleasant home at 55, Above Bar. It was linked to John's occupation as the Billiard Rooms proprietor, the baths and billiard rooms being behind their home. Thomas had taken up an apprenticeship as a plumber just before his father's death; but his mother, with four younger sons and a five year old daughter, Lucinda, to provide for, now worked as a servant at The Star Hotel in the High Street.

Now, with fresh responsibilities looming ahead, the newly wed young couple needed somewhere to live. Thomas was lodging in a boarding house, in Castle Square near the castle site and the Quaker Meeting House.[4] It would not be possible for Annie to move in with him there. Lodging house accommodation was intended chiefly for working men, although some were notorious disorderly houses (brothels) as well. Annie's parents lived in Cossack Street, in the Kingsland area of the town, a region generally accepted as run down and unhealthy, with privies and piped water shared between several families. Thomas and Annie moved into Vulcan Terrace in Chantry Road at the marshy end of the road, another poor and unpleasant part of the town. Near to the Docks, Chantry Road partially formed the approach to the Floating Bridge, which crossed the Itchen river here. This was a very low-lying part of the town, damp and prone to flooding from the tidal River Itchen.

Twenty years earlier, in a Public Health report from 1850, there had been many complaints about the stench from the mud around the Itchen Floating Bridge at low tide. This was due to a nearby sewage pipe outfall, which flooded across the landing place at high tide, leaving sewage deposited on the mud at low tide, where passengers had to walk when embarking and disembarking.[5] This was not a pleasant experience, yet it remained unaltered despite the many complaints from all those who had to use the Floating Bridge. It seems likely that even if the outfall had been diverted away from the landing place, the smell would have lingered on at low tide.

The surrounding streets and houses were mainly home to the dock workers and labourers. Conditions there prompted a series of outbursts, in the press, by a leading citizen, Mr Bicker-Caarten. His first letter to the *Southampton Times*, on 8 November 1890 painted a

FIGURE 1.1

Thomas Simmons (1849 -1934) trained as a plumber but ultimately ran a successful general store near the Docks.

(Private collection)

depressing picture of human misery for the dockers and their families:

> It was the same tale everywhere, want of work, want of money, little or no food, fires lit only for a short time to do the necessary cooking and then let out again... general helplessness and despondency as to how the wolf was to be kept from the door... This state of misery and destitution is chronic...It is caused by the lowness of the wages and by the casual nature of the work most of the people are employed in, by [the employers] utter want of responsibility for and interest in their labourers after they have paid them the small pittance for the few hours casual work, by there being two or three men for every job in the ranks of unskilled labour, and by the utter want of thrift on the part of the people themselves, caused by the conditions under which they...exist.

Rents were three or four shillings (15-20p) per week, often this was for one room, which had no adequate water supply. Some families were compelled to walk two hundred yards to a water standpipe; it was hardly surprising that most preferred to remain dirty at the end of a long day's toil, rather than carry buckets of water home for washing and other necessary purposes. Another correspondent reported that for people living in conditions like these 'it is no wonder that the glare of the public houses is such an attraction'.[6] Yet in this depressing environment two mission rooms did their best to raise both the morale and the morals of the people struggling to exist. The two clergymen of St James's Church, in Bernard Street, were rated as two of the hardest-working parsons in the town and that they were doing all they could to help the people.[7]

This then was the environment where Thomas and Annie started their married life together and it was here on 7 July 1873 their first son, George Thomas Simmons, was born. By the time their next child, Lilly, was born on 17 March 1875, the family had moved to a slightly larger and more comfortable house in Albert Street. This was to remain their main street of residence for most of their married life together, living in various houses, but at the same time running a general shop at 4, Albert Street.

The move to Albert Street did put them in a marginally more comfortable position. It is likely that the Vulcan Terrace accommodation had only been one room, so a house was a considerable improvement. It was situated behind the two main hotels that served the passengers for the liners, the smaller Canute Hotel and the South Western Hotel which sheltered the platforms of the Terminus railway station under its large porchway.

FIGURE 1.2

Hannah (Annie) Simmons (1856-1928) was to give birth to sixteen children, four of whom died before they started school.

The two hotels catered for two very different classes of passenger. The South Western which, with its commanding corner frontage, aimed to cater for the First Class and perhaps some Second Class travellers, while the Canute served those of more modest means. Their differences were clearly shown in their two advertisements in the local street directories. The South Western proclaimed its attributes as including its position opposite the Docks, with entrances from both platforms of the Terminus station and was 'most convenient for passengers arriving or departing by the steamers using this port and is replete with every comfort and convenience'. These included hot and cold shower baths, and a good billiard room. Its marbled hallway had a modern lift to all floors and suction points (connected to a large pump in the basement) distributed around the building ensured efficient cleaning, by plugging a vacuum cleaning hose direct into the suction points. By contrast the Canute advertisement stressed its proximity to the station only one hundred yards distant and exactly opposite the Dock gates. Its main facilities were its views across the Docks and even as far as the Isle of Wight. As was usual, the extreme poverty of the surrounding area was adjacent to the extreme luxury offered by the larger hotel. Many of those employed by the hotels would come from and live in the poorer streets behind them. For these workers trained to be 'invisible' in the hotel, the contrast between their own living conditions and those of the hotel guests must have seemed grossly unfair. With such a system of inequality, it is perhaps not surprising that so many working class people opted to emigrate via the liners and start a new life in America.

In their new environment the Simmons family grew rapidly. Altogether Thomas and Annie had sixteen children, although four did not reach adulthood and died before the age of five. Although this was not an unusual situation, the survival rate of the Simmons children appears to have been better than for many in the area. The causes of death were predictable; infectious diseases like measles and diphtheria took their toll while bronchitis in the damp conditions in many homes, was almost an inevitable outcome of any initially minor cold infection. The death certificate for their third child aged six months, gives an indication just how protracted illness could be, in a pre-antibiotic era. Diagnosed with 'suppressed measles' which continued for eleven days, this then developed into bronchitis which lasted for a further fourteen days, before the baby's eventual death.

As was usual the babies were born at home or, perhaps more unusually, at the home of a friend or relative. This may have been the case with some of the oldest Simmons children. At least two of Annie's first babies were born at another address in Paget Street, but her own home address is given as different from the birth address. The inference has to be that there was an unofficial 'midwife' operating in Paget Street and Annie preferred to use her services and premises, while her (Annie's) other children were still very young. It was also traditional for birth to be a concern for women only, so perhaps the move was intended to exclude Thomas, as well as the toddlers, from the scene of birth. Although middle-class Victorian and Edwardian society maintained a prudish attitude towards sex, which often left their own women in a state of ignorance, the desperate struggle for survival amongst the lower strata of society meant that some women developed considerable skills in midwifery; 'lying-in' for births and 'laying-out' of bodies after a death. The call to a knowledgeable neighbour was still common practice until after the Second World War and the establishment of the National Health Service.

As shown by Thomas's own baptism being delayed until he was three years old, it was not unusual for families to delay the cost of baptising their children and then to have two or three christened at the same time. So it was that George, their firstborn, was not baptised at St Mary's Church until February 1876, when he was two and a half years old. However, to make the ceremony worthwhile, his younger sister Lilly Eliza, aged under one year, was baptised at the same time. At this time Thomas was described as 'labourer'. Five years later in 1881, he preferred to call himself 'Plumber's labourer' when the census enumerator enquired about his profession - status was all important, when dealing with officialdom. Baptism for the growing family seems to have continued on a rather random basis, until after the death of their seventh child, William John, in 1882. Aged two months, he was baptised (the baptismal register is marked 'clinical') and buried a few days later. It may be that the Rector of St Mary's was exasperated by Thomas's and Annie's apparently casual approach towards their children's spiritual care and took them to task over the matter. Were they really acting as responsible parents? Were the children's deaths intended as a warning to them and a reminder of their responsibilities? It is hard to judge what their feelings were, but in February 1883 Thomas and Annie had young Annie aged five, Lucy aged three and Albert just turned two, all baptised at the same time. After this all subsequent children were taken to the font on a more regular basis.

On 16 May 1887, Frederick Charles Simmons, was born at 36, Albert Street, the sixth surviving child in what was ultimately to be a family of eleven surviving children. He was born into a household which consisted not only of his parents and older siblings, but also his mother's brother William Minns and his family. Thus, the two young families were crammed into the little four-roomed house, while the shop at the front provided them with some means of support.

Thomas was describing himself as shopkeeper at this period. Over the next few years he gave his profession variously as grocer, greengrocer and general dealer. He always stated that he was both self-employed and an employer. Annie by contrast, is more prosaic in her description and simply called him a Dock Labourer, when she registered Fred's birth.

No doubt Annie and the children would have been 'employed' in the shop whenever possible. It was legal for children to be employed from the age of ten years at this time. With the rather erratic schooling arrangements offered locally, there were plenty of opportunities for the children to be gainfully employed by their father as well as their Uncle William who was a paper hanger and painter. Taken with Thomas's plumbing skills, the joint family may have run another business as house decorators, in addition to the shop. As well as these suggestions (general dealer, dock labourer and plumber), a comment made by Fred in a letter written from his parents' home, suggests that another line of employment may have been available to the family as well. In the letter, Fred says he had been working on another ship in dock all day. If this was the case, then perhaps Thomas together with his family, helped to victual or 'fit out' some ships before each voyage.

Whatever the truth about Thomas's working arrangements, there can be no doubt that he and Annie worked hard to provide for their family and raise them as honest, hardworking people. The Docks provided many opportunities for those willing to be flexible and Thomas was certainly adaptable.

Annie and Thomas had been married just three years after the 1870 Education Act, when free education was made a compulsory right for all children. They took full advantage of this facility for their family.

CHAPTER 2

SCHOOLDAYS

New Simmons children arrived in the family with daunting regularity and, with the same regularity endeavoured to obtain an elementary education at the Eastern Board School in Anglesea Terrace, in St Mary's parish. This was just a ten minute walk away from their home and in 1892 Fred, aged five, in company with his older siblings, trotted off to school to do battle with the three Rs - reading, (w)riting and (a)rithmetic.

This was the same year the Headmistress of the Infants, Miss Darling, expressed concern about the need of equipment for the Mixed Infants - there were not enough desks. Children had to kneel on the floor leaning on forms, to do their copy writing; the window blinds in the room were completely worn out and needed replacing; a strong lockable cupboard was required and a new set of fire irons. A reminder that classrooms were heated by pot-bellied coal stoves and it was the responsibility of the teachers to keep the fire alight.

The lack of desks was not helped by the large class numbers; Class 1 (the Babies) had fifty-five children when Fred joined it. In 1896 the situation remained unchanged and Miss Darling was forced to borrow forms from the kitchen for the children to work on.

The poverty of the area meant that sometimes children did not come to school because they had no shoes to wear. On one occasion the girls and teachers collected money for a new pair of boots for Daisy Candy, 'with the left one built up with cork for her short leg'; these cost 12s 6d (62½p). It was recorded that she was in school the next day wearing her new boots. Daisy was not the only child to come to school poorly clad and the staff maintained baskets of old clothes, at the school, to give their needy pupils something to wear.

With three schools on the site; the Mixed Infants (5-7 years), the Girls' School (8-13/14 years) and the Boys' School (8-13/14 years), overcrowding was rife. Originally built by the Peninsular and Oriental Steam Packet Company for employees' children, the school had never been intended for the five hundred children now attending lessons there. The single storey building housed the boys' school in one wing; the girls' school in the other and the infants school in the centre section, between the two wings. The house for the Master was integrated into the building, together with his garden. Washrooms, toilets and two dining rooms for the children were also on the site.

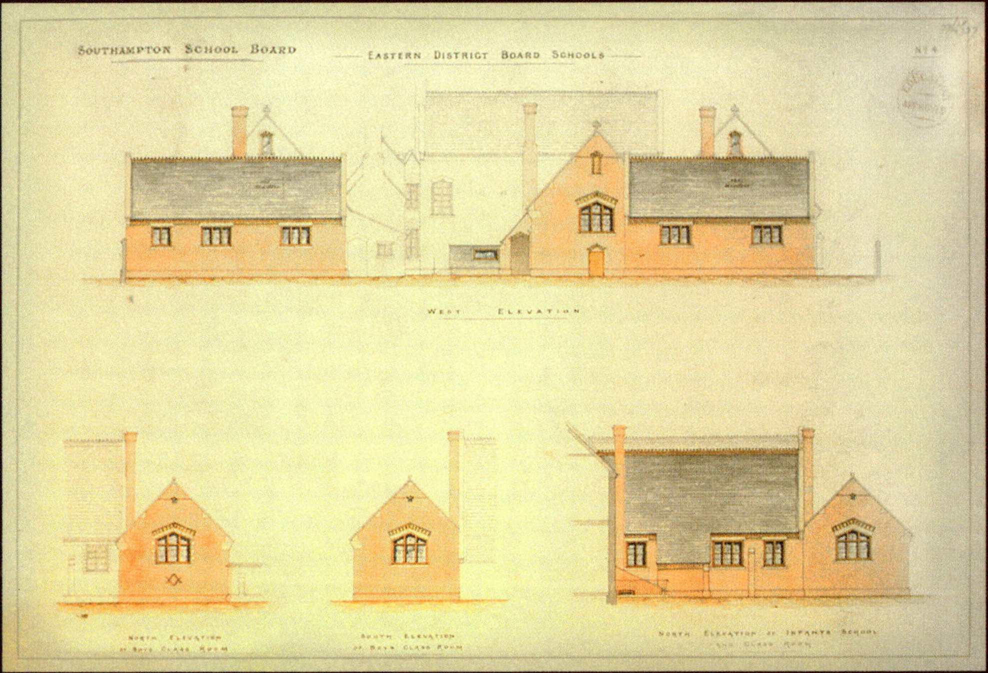
SOUTHAMPTON SCHOOL BOARD
EASTERN DISTRICT BOARD SCHOOLS
WEST ELEVATION
NORTH ELEVATION OF BOYS CLASS ROOM
SOUTH ELEVATION OF BOYS CLASS ROOM
NORTH ELEVATION OF INFANTS SCHOOL AND CLASS ROOM

After 1870 the school had been taken over by the Corporation and became the Eastern Board School. From that time on there were always problems about staff and their suitability; the school managers were never slow to sack teachers who were proving unsuitable, but not always so eager to appoint replacements. Miss Smith, the Headmistress of the Girls' school, in a letter to the School Managers in 1890, does not mince her words:

> The class of children attending this school is bad. A large number come from homes in which they not only have no right moral training, but are constantly in the midst of vice and depravity. Such being the case, young Pupil Teachers are not capable of working the classes as they ought to be worked and the results are not as good as could be wished.
> May I ask you to consider the advisability of having an Ex P[upil] T[eacher] instead of another young P[upil] T[eacher].

Besides the young inexperienced Pupil Teachers, who were usually about thirteen years of age, the staff used some of the pupils as Monitors, to teach the younger children. Some Monitors could be as young as seven or eight, and each received a shilling (5p) per week - a useful addition to some household budgets no doubt – but even this small payment had to be approved by the School Managers.

Staff salaries were set by the Managers and all staff, including the Head Teachers, had to apply for a raise (usually five pounds) each year. There was no guarantee they would get it, even after serving many years at the school. Average salaries for assistant teachers were between sixty and eighty pounds per annum, an amount which appears to be less than the school caretaker received.

The constant absences of pupils and staff reflected the deprivation of the area. Some staff were scarcely better off than their pupils and it was very rare that all staff were present for two successive days. Even at the beginning of term such an occurrence needed special mention in the school logbook. Staff were assailed by a variety of ailments - sore throats were common, quinsy, bronchitis, inflammation of the lungs, poisoned fingers and neuralgia were all given as reasons for staff absences. Tom James's mother, as a teacher at Redbridge School in Millbrook, got copper poisoning from handling school dinner money. Concern about health was always a priority amongst families and friends - the greeting, 'How are you?' was not intended as a politeness but a genuine query.

Only more serious illnesses were reported for the pupils, usually because some sort of quarantine was needed to prevent the illness spreading. An outbreak of diphtheria was reported in the school during 1899 and Fred's sister Minnie was absent in April 1903 because there was diphtheria at home. Just two years earlier the few cases of typhoid noted on 30 August 1901 had become a serious outbreak by October the same year.

Besides problems with pupils' truancy and sickness amongst staff, the school suffered constant disruptions due to half-day holidays for a great variety of reasons - VIP visitors generously gave the children extra 'days off' and there were various regular 'treats' when the school closed early, for example for the duration of St Mary's Fair and Chapel Fair.[8] On these days the school opened early after lunch at 1pm and closed at 3.15pm. It was claimed that by this method a few children did attend in the afternoon.

Other closures occurred for swimming, athletics, football and other sports tournaments or lessons. On the afternoon of the Cycling Carnival in 1897, held in the grounds of Westwood House near the Avenue, there were only one hundred and seven children in the school out of more than five hundred pupils. The Agricultural Show, also at Westwood House estate, was another popular excuse for truancy, but during the week of the School Board exhibition the school was directed to only open for the mornings. Presumably the children and staff were supposed to attend the exhibition each afternoon. For the Queen's Jubilee in 1897, the school was given the whole week off, but all the classes met at the school on the Wednesday, before walking to the Common for their Jubilee Treat.

Small wonder that with such a variety of school closures, staff absences, overcrowding and lack of equipment, any education the children gained would be very elementary indeed. Nonetheless the staff continued to battle on, doing their utmost to provide their charges with the basics of reading, writing and arithmetic.

As well as these skills, efforts were made to provide the children with an introduction to music. Fred became part of the school's team of handbell ringers, which must have been quite an innovation in such a deprived area. At the same time, singing was regarded as an important part of the curriculum, for all classes. Even so, the harmoniums were often in need of repair and not considered of any use.[9] As preparation for their expected roles in society, girls were given needlework and cookery lessons, whilst the boys did some woodwork.

Physical health was not overlooked either, with regular 'drill' (Physical Education) lessons. The equipment provided was limited; the boys had hoops and poles while the girls used fans for 'fan drill'. This entailed a strictly choreographed series of marching manoeuvres, with the girls marching in lines, which crossed and threaded between one another. This was

FIGURE 2.3

Fred's First Class swimming certificate. Schools gave certificates of encouragement for a variety of achievements, including attendance and punctuality.

FIGURE 2.4

Fred's 1898 attendance certificate shows that William Spranger was Chairman of the Board. Spranger rescued Tudor House, restored it and gave it to the town as a museum.

then followed by a sequence of actions using fans to express a variety of emotions. The fans cost the school two shillings and ninepence (13.5p) per dozen (twelve) from Robert Russell's fancy goods shop in East Street. Whilst the first section of the drill can be seen to be of some value to the girls' health and memory skills, the use of fans could be expected to be well outside the experience of these children and hardly suitable for any likely employment they would obtain. Nature walks were encouraged and the children were also marched off to the boys' and girls' baths for swimming lessons, under the auspices of the Elementary Schools' Swimming Club.

Altogether the picture is more like a Ragged School rather than an official Board School and attainment levels were not much better - the staff were especially congratulated when the School Inspectors regraded the school, from 'Poor/Failed' to 'Fair'.

This then was the chaotic environment where Fred, received his education, learning to read and write kneeling on the floor; leaning on borrowed forms in hopelessly overcrowded and mostly unheated classrooms; learning his music scales with a broken harmonium; drilling in the playground with hoops and a pole for equipment and marching to the baths for swimming lessons.

By the time Fred started at the school, however, Miss Smith's impassioned letter of December 1890 had borne some fruit. The Rector of St Mary's Church and a lady, Miss Bradby, had joined the School Managers by the end of November 1892 and the Registrar of Births, Marriages and Deaths, Mr Hunt, was checking the class registers on a regular basis.

The Rector took it upon himself to pay unannounced visits to the school and to sit in on classes. No doubt this was also a useful way of finding new choirboys for the Church. Perhaps this was how Fred joined the church choir - scrubbed up, he was probably quite presentable with his fair hair, blue eyes and slight build. Popular family tradition maintains that when he was older, a congregation member wanted to send him for proper singing lessons to train his voice. Annie his mother, refused, saying she did not want him getting 'ideas above his station'. 'Class' was important even at the lower ends of society.

By the time he was thirteen, Fred was the eldest of the children left at home and it is easy to imagine him taking charge of his younger brothers and sisters. Over the years he probably had gained considerable child-care skills within the ever-increasing Simmons and Minns extended family unit. More importantly he was probably a useful errand boy for his father's business as well, running messages to other shopkeepers, delivering items to customers, learning to communicate with a variety of people, knowing when to be respectful, learning when to keep quiet and when he could let his sense of humour loose.

And so Fred's schooldays and childhood passed. What had he gained to serve him into adult life? Incredibly he left school with a love of reading and writing. His handwriting was neat and tidy, even with the notoriously messy 'dip' pens which were used. Thanks to the choir he sang well, he was popular with people, a good swimmer and could ride a bike. The school found places for many of its pupils, including Fred's eldest sister Maud. It seems unlikely, however, that they placed Fred, given that he was probably already working for his father. Children could legally work from the age of ten and apprenticeships usually started at fourteen. These lasted for seven years, until the individual was twenty-one when they officially 'came of age', thus becoming an adult and responsible for their own destiny.

Fred seems to have worked with his father for the next couple of years, possibly until his younger brother Bertie, was old enough to take his place. Then at last he could satisfy his wanderlust. No doubt this had been encouraged by visits to the Docks (just half a mile away) with his father and hearing sailors' tales of South America and the West Indies. So, claiming to be sixteen, Fred went to sea as Captain Tindall's Servant, on the Royal Mail ship *Clyde*. It was August 1902, he was bound for Brazil and would be away for six weeks. The great adventure had begun.

CHAPTER 3

WINIFRED

Winifred had never seen her grandfather so angry. John Newton Lucraft was beside himself with rage. His anger, hurt and disappointment filled the tiny cottage, where he and her grandmother lived.

"Martha", Grandmother was speaking to her mother, "Why don't we take the children for a walk, while the men discuss their business?"

They all knew this was not to be a discussion but an ultimatum, from father to son. Life was about to change dramatically for the three children, Eveline, William and the youngest, Winifred.

Eveline had been baptised here in the village church at Broadclyst, in Devon. People knew the family, even though they had moved away some years ago. John Martin Lucraft, the children's father, had grown up in the village and attended the village school, before undertaking his grocery apprenticeship.

The family's progress from the cottage, past Town End Farm, where many of John Newton Lucraft's barrels were in use, up Town Hill and through the little village, was punctuated by frequent stops and introductions. Winifred was conscious of her mother and grandmother keeping up a cheerful appearance to the many enquiries about their health and business. Eventually they arrived at the churchyard. The two women found a seat and sat down in the autumn sunshine.

"Eveline, take William and Winifred to see the Church while your mother and I have a talk".

Eveline felt a little aggrieved by this command from Grandmother. At sixteen, she felt old enough to be included in whatever was happening. As the three children started to walk away, they heard their usually quiet and gentle grandmother speaking vehemently,

" This will be the last time, Martha. He won't help any more. To be honest, I don't think he wants to see John ever again".

What *was* happening at the cottage?

* * *

John Newton Lucraft had been a cautious and thrifty businessman throughout his life. He was well respected as the village cooper, making iron hooped barrels that were used by the cider trade and other storage purposes, as well.

FIGURE 3.1

Winifred Lucraft aged about thirteen. When girls were aged between fifteen and sixteen they were expected to pin their hair up.

Over the years he had made many business contacts and worked hard to gain a reputation for good work, honesty and reliability throughout the area. He had even successfully weathered the disastrous Broadclyst fire in May 1870, which had destroyed sixty of the seventy-eight houses in the village. Some years prior to the fire he had leased a row of eight cottages in Exeter Road, from Sir Thomas Acland, of Killerton House and these had been completely gutted by the fire. Under the terms of the agreement, John Lucraft was liable for their re-building, despite the lease only having a short time left to run. The repairs cost him most of his savings and caused some hardship for the family.

This had been a terrible setback but thrift, hard work and the support of Annie, his wife of nearly fifty years, had seen them through. They had worked hard to regain their financial position and find the hundred pounds necessary for their son's apprenticeship as a grocer. John Newton Lucraft took a quiet pride in the family's local standing and comfortable, if modest lifestyle.

So what was wrong with his son? Hadn't he tried to give him the same values? Hadn't he paid for the seven-year apprenticeship needed to train him as a grocer - always a good solid trade? Hadn't he paid to set him up in his first business, in Dartmouth? Hadn't he paid the debts when the business failed? Hadn't he set him up in a new business in Ilfracombe? And now that had failed as well. He and Annie were too old to have this kind of worry now.

He might as well face up to it, his son John Martin Lucraft, was an irresponsible, feckless drunkard.

The interview was short and painful for both men.

The father reiterated all the values he had tried to instil into his son; the money invested in the son's future, his first business, the debts paid to avoid his bankruptcy, setting him up in another business, only to see the pattern of drunkenness and irresponsibility repeated once more.

"You do realise that I would have let you become a bankrupt? It was your sisters who paid your debts and persuaded me, against my better judgement, to give you one last chance. Have you no self-respect; sponging on women? You have a wife and children. Do you want to see them sent to the workhouse? This is your last chance. It is only for your family's sake I have arranged this. I have no particular wish to ever see you again."

John Martin Lucraft left the little cottage and went in search of his family. The clear sky and weak sunshine started to revive his spirits. By the time he had been greeted by a few villagers and located his family in the churchyard, his usual irrepressible, ebullient charm had returned.

"Father has found me a position, working in a shop - in Southampton!" he announced. Relief swept away some of the lines of tension which had been on Martha's face during the last difficult months. His mother only gave a silent, tight smile.

* * *

It is doubtful that John Martin Lucraft had any idea just how much careful consideration his father must have put into the choice of location for this new position.

John Newton Lucraft was a man who assessed the possible outcomes of his actions. There were a number of criteria he needed to fulfil and possibly the most important was to get his son well away from the area. Too close and news of yet another business scandal would soon be known and possibly affect the son's new position. He had heard that the growing port of Southampton was booming, with the railway and docks drawing workers into the town from all over the country. Manpower was needed to build and maintain the development of roads, railways, docks and shipping. The integrated services of trains, docks and ships drew visitors into the town to stay at fashionable hotels, which would also require manpower. A business sited near the dock area, where most of the workers lived, must be prosperous and working for someone else might just bring his wayward son to his senses.

There were other considerations as well - the futures of the three children. Eveline was already learning the grocery trade, she could either continue with that or see what was available in Southampton. William had hopes of joining the Army. If he changed his mind, a career would have to be found for him. Opportunities for him would exist in the town as well, carpentry perhaps. Winifred, or 'Tot' as she was affectionately known in the family, was skilful with her needle; perhaps she could take up a trade useful to all those wealthy visitors, coming to Southampton. Dressmakers and milliners would surely be needed to ensure the lady passengers had the very latest fashions to take on board ship, for their sea voyages.

Southampton seemed to offer the right possibilities for a fresh start and so, in 1897, John Martin Lucraft was settled into his new position with Thomas Hayward, in Millbank Street. The location of Hayward's grocery shop hardly seems to have been conducive to anyone attempting to withstand the temptations of 'the demon drink' - on the opposite corner was *The Cooper's Arms* and next door was William Warner, a beer retailer. Just around the corner however, in Bond Street, the Church Army was ready to come to the rescue if needed. Notwithstanding temptation, just a year later John Lucraft was negotiating for the lease of Mrs Cove's Coffee Tavern, in Guildhall Terrace, when she vacated it. Situated on the corner of Bond Street, it was just five doors away from Thomas Hayward's shop.

FIGURE 3.2

Broadclyst church where Lucrafts had been baptised and buried for several generations.

FIGURE 3.3

Cob and thatch cottages nearly six hundred years old across the village green.

Since John was a grocer by trade, it seems a little strange that when he opened this new shop initially, it was listed in the local directories as a 'colorman and hardware store' . Now he sold and possibly mixed paint for customers, as well as some tools and household hardware. A change of trade which all sounds reminiscent of a modern Do-It-Yourself store!

Located in the heart of industrial Northam, the shop was surrounded by gas and oil storage tanks, timber yards, shipbuilding and shipping wharves, an iron foundry, linseed oil factory, margarine factory and underground sewage works; the gasworks were not far away and neither was the workhouse. The locality could not have been more different from the quiet little town of Ilfracombe, with its small yachts and fishing vessels to service and fresh sea breezes, instead of smoke laden air. Due to the curve in the river, Northam was surrounded on three sides by water, and on the westward side it was separated from neighbouring Newtown, by the railway line and engine sheds. Largely responsible for the dirty work necessary to maintain the town, and preferably forgotten by many people, Northam was frequently referred to as 'the Cinderella of Southampton'.[10]

Unfortunately, during the deliberations about the location for John's new start, no one had been aware of the unemployment which was rife in the town. The Commissioners of the Poor said that the poor and unemployed flocked to the town like 'homing pigeons'.[11] No doubt it was a similar story in other towns offering potential opportunities for work, but Southampton may have suffered more than others because the variety of opportunities seemed greater, for those seeking employment. It was not a situation likely to turn the failing fortunes of the Lucraft family around. The sign on the outside of the shop was quickly repainted to become 'Cash Grocer'.

The move to Southampton was certain to impact on the children's lives, so that they all followed very different career paths, but not always the one they wished to pursue. Maud, Martha's eldest daughter and half-sister to the other siblings, was a regular visitor to the shop and family home. After working as a governess to the wealthy banking Baring family, she was now living in London and working for the Church Missionary Society. William Lucraft, their son, had joined the army and was sent to South Africa to join the Boer War as expected, but luckily the war ended before he went to the front line. He returned from South Africa, not only with tales of travel and adventure but also, in need of a trade. A position with a bakery filled the need and ultimately took him on his travels again, as a ship's baker.

In the meantime Martha, had been looking for a suitable school for Winifred, her youngest daughter, to finish her education. No doubt Martha threw her hands up in horror at

FIGURE 3.4

Workmen clearing the gutted row of cottages that cost John Newton Lucraft most of his savings.

FIGURE 3.5

The cottages as they are now in 2012.

the local establishments - Northam School and the Eastern Board School. For her youngest daughter to go to either was unthinkable. A small private school for young ladies was found for Winifred to spend the last few years of her education. This was a fact which rankled with her elder sister Eveline, who had dreamt of being a teacher, but instead had been expected to work in her father's shop at Ilfracombe and continued to do so here, at Northam.

One of Eveline's duties in the shop was setting and clearing the mouse traps. With produce stored in sacks or canvas bags, it was always vulnerable to attack by vermin and most shops had infestations of rodents; the Lucraft shop was no exception. However, the mice did have their uses.

A young man, Will Mallett, called into the shop one day, on his way to work and asked if he could have any mice they caught. Martha was aghast, but Eveline was intrigued,

"What do you want dead mice for?"

"Well, I've found a baby owl that had fallen out of its nest somewhere, and I need to feed it."

"Ugh! How horrid!" was Eveline's reply.

"Oh, no – that's what they eat, it's quite natural. Honest! I've already kept the owl alive for the last few days with bread and milk, but now it needs proper food and I noticed you throwing the dead mice away yesterday, so thought you might help."

Feeling flattered that she had been noticed, by this young man, Eveline agreed to maintain a supply of mice for the owl. Will's frequent visits resulted in Eveline being invited to tea, to 'meet the owl'. Their friendship deepened and eventually they married early in 1905 – whether the owl went to the wedding is uncertain, but it remained a family pet. After its demise, it was stuffed and mounted, to remain as a cherished family heirloom.

Whatever the ultimate outcomes would be, for the moment the Lucraft family appeared to be on an even keel and stability had been restored.

* * *

So it had come about that the Simmons and Lucraft families lived within two miles of one another, but how did our two young people meet one another? What events, circumstances or coincidences brought them together? It is possible a number of contributory factors came into effect.

The arrival of the Lucraft paint and hardware store in the local area must have been useful for the Minns family decorating business. If, as seems likely, Fred Simmons was acting as his father's errand boy, he could have become a useful link between the Lucraft hardware shop

FIGURE 3.6

John Newton Lucraft's cottage where he lived with his family.

FIGURE 3.7

The Lucraft family shortly after coming to Southampton. The children left to right, Winifred, William and Eveline. Seated John Martin Lucraft and his wife, Martha.

(Private collection)

and his Uncle William Minns. Moreover, 'Uncle' Ezekiel Simmons was living in Bond Street near the Lucraft shop, giving another reason for Fred to be in the area.

Fred, then a teenager, may have taken messages between the two shopkeeper fathers as well. No doubt they shared common problems and could have supplied goods for one another's customers. Alternatively, John Lucraft's usual convivial habits may have caused him to strike up a friendship with Thomas Simmons in one of the many local hostelries. Certainly a friendly acquaintance seems to have developed between the two families, despite their different backgrounds. Sundays could have seen a variety of Minns, Simmons and Lucraft family members greeting one another at St Mary's Church, where Fred was still a choir member.

However the contact was made, it seems to have been natural for Fred and Winifred to strike up a friendship; there was after all, only a few months difference in their ages. Over the years Winifred had built up a small collection of postcards sent by her family and friends. So when Fred took up his first position on the *RMS Clyde* in 1902, he probably offered to send her postcards from the places he visited. A long correspondence was to follow with results that would reverberate through the following decades.

Lucraft shop at Northam (Private collection)

CHAPTER 4

LETTERS HOME

" Letter for Miss Lucraft," announced the postman as he put it on the shop counter.

Eveline looked up, surprised. She left the tea she was blending and picked up the letter.

"It's for Tot!"

"Really?" said Martha, as she weighed out the customer's sugar into the blue sugar paper bag.

"It's probably young Fred," she continued, "I think Tot had given up hoping he'd ever remember; it will be a nice surprise for her, when she gets home from school".

"Just look at it, Mother. I don't know *how* it's managed to arrive safely. He seems to have great faith in the mail ships and Southampton postal service".

Eveline had every right to be scathing about the 'letter'. A packet of three postcards, it was held together by a piece of stamp edging wrapped around one side and the stamp stuck round the opposite side. The postcard sandwiched in the middle wasn't stuck to anything.

When Winifred returned from school and opened up the three cards, after rearranging them, she had a panoramic view of Madeira, showing the hills in the centre and the huddle of white houses stretching along the shoreline. The message inside was awkward and brief, but conveyed some of the concerns that would dominate this long distance friendship.

> Have now a chance of 5-10 minutes smoke. So please be a good girl and dont forget to write.
>
> Yours with kind regards etc
> Fred

Several letters speak of problems finding a few minutes spare time to write, or give instructions about how to keep in touch for example 'don't write to New York slow boat.' An internal mail system existed between ships. The crews used the mailbags carried by returning vessels, from various shipping lines, hence some letters are marked *Via French Mails*. In others, Fred names specific ships he is using to send the letter, including the *St Louis*, and *Mauretania*.

The instruction to Winifred 'not to write to New York slow boat' meant her letter would not reach him before he sailed for home himself. On another occasion he says she can write as soon as she gets his letter and send hers, via Cunard. They both must have developed an

FIGURE 4.1

Fred Simmons aged about eighteen. After his death Winifred had a large copy, of the photograph made, which she kept hung on the wall.

(Simmons archive)

FIGURE 4.2

This panoramic view of Madeira was the first 'letter' that Winifred received from Fred, probably as an addition to her postcard collection.

(Simmons archive)

intimate knowledge of shipping movements and how to use them to their own advantage, in their efforts to keep in contact.

Understandably with long gaps between letters, there are ongoing references to issues about finance and the overriding concerns about one another's health. This latter concern must be seen within the context of an era with no public healthcare and the prevalence of highly contagious infections. Ships could be especially vulnerable in such circumstances. A local newspaper report in 1904, records how contaminated water taken on board a British ship in Rotterdam, spread enteric fever on board and caused the ship to be removed from port.

Reading the letters through it's apparent that Fred trusted Winifred implicitly with his affairs and he is soon sending her money, to keep for his return. Often stilted and formal, the messages are brief, but in 1905-06, there is a subtle change in the tone. Fred starts sending messages of regard and affection to 'all at home'.

This was a period of upheaval in the life of the Lucraft family. John Lucraft was facing bankruptcy once again and these messages of regard seem to have been Fred's naturally supportive nature manifesting itself, to show his solidarity with them all. As might be expected, he was equally supportive of his own family members; asking Winifred to come to their home on one occasion, when he wanted to remain there to help his mother, Annie, who was unwell.

In another letter he tells of meeting up with two of his brothers, Jim and Ern, in New York, giving one of them a ball and needing to get the boots 'over' as well. Possibly this was because his brother's ship's crew wanted to play football - a popular activity when a ship's crew had free time in port. Meanwhile Fred and Jim went to see a play together, *Captain Spinney at the North Pole*. Fred remarks laconically 'it was a fair play, but I don't think I'll trouble it again'.

Through these letters we also gain indirect evidence of John Lucraft's affection and concern for his youngest daughter. Two letters give clues to the relationship, not only between father and daughter but also between Fred and 'Dad'; obviously the two men were able to discuss their concerns with one another and John Lucraft seems to have tried to reassure Fred that he would take care of Winifred during Fred's absence;

> ...all I want to know is that you are well. How is Dad, I hope he was handy if he was wanted I know he cant do enough...
>
> ...I suppose Dad is away by now and that you both (Winifred and Martha) miss him...

There seems to have been a genuine regard and affection between the two men. Fred brings back 'baccy' and makes a teasing remark about 'Dad' missing his 'torch' - apparently a standing joke about John Lucraft's pipe. A much later letter bemoans the fact that John Lucraft had not been available to sign on for the *Oceanic*, as the ship was short of five men. The next letter, while he was still on this trip, expands on his frustration at waiting for the older man to come to the quay to collect some money. Fred had wanted John Lucraft to take some money home to Winifred; other crewmen also took the opportunity to pass money on, via their colleague's contact. Understandably Fred sounds a bit peeved, when he relates that he waited until 11.35pm, before dashing across to the White Star Laundry and asking the manageress to take the money for the crew's families; on his return to the ship he was told that John Lucraft was waiting on the quay for him, presumably after the public houses had all closed. Too late - Fred had his duties to carry out, now.

And so the correspondence continued, across the miles and across the years, despite the many unavoidable long silences between letters, they persevered for ten eventful years.

R.M.S.P. "TAGUS."

CHAPTER 5

A LIFE ON THE OCEAN WAVE

> "Shake a leg! Come on now you tired hunks, up now and lets 'ave ya!"
> 'This was our greeting on Sunday at 4.45 a.m. Out of our 'bug-walks' we got and our orders were to bathbrick the Saloon out, then we were finished for the day.[12] At 7.30 a.m. we had finished the Saloon and a few of us went to do a bit of fishing. After about one hour we managed to catch enough fish for the cat's breakfast, so went on board for our own. We did not enjoy it, because it was leather and worms, which in other words means Royal Mail steak and macaroni. We all got over or under it and those that were not ill came for a little more fishing.
> 'After a time, fishing got too dry, so one of the Hunks (Stewards) proposed bathing. Six of us agreed and we spent 2½ hours in the water, when we did have some fine fun!'

Not content with writing letters, Fred also wrote accounts of some events which had made an impression on him, in an exercise book The above extract refers to a day spent ashore, after he had joined the *RMS Atrato* on the West Indies mail run. These were long trips, lasting seven to eight weeks and sometimes included trading voyages around the various islands. There were many ships, however, from different ports doing similar trips and it was not unusual for seamen to leave one ship and join another for a short period, in order to visit other islands. Fred was not one to miss such an opportunity and 'hitch-hiked' to Jamaica from Trinidad, via the *Solent* and *Trent*, before rejoining the *Atrato*, to return home. He gives us an insight and flavour of the West Indies, from the account of a day's shore leave at Savanña de Mer during his trip in May 1905.

Their water games are probably familiar to most people, floating and swimming with logs and 'pyramids', which entailed climbing on top of one another's shoulders, before diving in. Their sport ended when one dived into water that was too shallow and grazed his head slightly. They returned on board for lunch, which was 'passable' and then the suggestion was put that they go ashore to look for orchids - such antics were not unusual in an age before conservation became an issue.

'An old fellow met us as we came off the pier, he was our guide. He took us to

FIGURE 5.1

Southampton High Street, showing Capital and Labour awning next to the Dolphin Hotel.

FIGURE 5.2

Enlargement of the awning showing lettering more clearly.

(F.G.O. Stuart)

> his hut and we helped ourselves to knives and choppers. Then we all started and got to the bush about 2.15 p.m. We had to plough our way through and we quite enjoyed it. One would be falling over the stump of a tree and another would be swearing because a branch of a tree had hit him in the face.
>
> 'Orchids!' 'Where?' 'Up in that tree!' So then we started to cut the tree down and hot work we found it.
>
> At last the tree fell and we cut the orchids off and went on our way. We saw several wild animals, small snakes and lizards.
>
> "Simmo! Where are you? There, another orchid up that tree!'
>
> Taking my knife, I went up the tree and started to cut the orchid down, when a slight rustling in the bushes below me made me start. I came down with a run and didn't stop till I reached the bottom. I was a bit scratched and found that the thing which made me jump was a young bird.
>
> 'We got a few more orchids and then we made our way home. Reaching the guide's hut we sat down and had a drink. Looking at the Atrato we thought of all the good people at home going to church!'

Such high spirits would seem to strike a chord with most people's youth. The group of probably rather drunk, young men finished up by all falling in the water, fully clothed. Hoping to sneak back on board before being seen by any of the officers, in such a dishevelled state, they had the misfortune to be caught by 'the Boss'.

> 'Had a good day by the look of you', he said.
>
> 'No more leave for you, my holy terrors'

Discipline was strict even under the eye of an understanding ship's Master.

Fred ends the day's account by dryly signing himself off as the 'Star of the Atrato', which seems to verify that he was entertaining the passengers on a regular basis.

* * *

The teenager's life had changed radically when he went to sea - this was where his real education began. Fred had joined the *Clyde*, on August 9 1902 as Captain Tindall's servant and embarked on his first six week mail run to Brazil. He would be away until October. This trip was an initiation into the traditions of the Merchant Navy.

Merchant seamen had for hundreds of years been able to sell their services in an open market, they were not tied to either a particular shipping line or ship, although many of them did become regular crewmembers for a single vessel. They could expect their food to be provided on board (complaints and suspicions about rations were traditional), but they were expected to outfit themselves prior to a voyage with uniform, hammock and bedding, including a straw mattress (known as a 'donkey's breakfast') and their own eating utensils. These items, together with any personal effects, were kept in the seaman's own sea chest to be stored in the crew's quarters.

Working as a steward either in the cabins or the saloons, caused special problems for his uniform waistcoats. These were white with brass buttons. However, even the most experienced stewards sometimes had various soups, stews or drinks spilt down their uniform. Stains could be washed out of the material, but frequently the hot fluids reacted with the brass of the buttons and tarnished them. Such scruffiness would not be tolerated by either Captain, or passengers. Fred quickly learned that stewards bought the best quality buttons, for their uniform waistcoats. These buttons were made of brass, but with a special non-tarnishable metal surface applied to them. Apart from a wipe off to remove any spillages, these buttons never needed cleaning, unlike the brass buttons of the officers' uniforms.

There were a number of uniform providers in Southampton, the most well known being Millers in Oxford Street. They were also the most prestigious and therefore, more expensive than Fred could afford. He favoured the more modest Capital and Labour Outfitters, next door to the Dolphin Hotel in the High Street. Although cheaper than others, the standard of their clothes and the quality of their buttons was very good. Being more expensive than the plain brass ones, these were always removable, using a split pin through the button shank, on the reverse of the waistcoat, to hold them in place. They were then easily removed to a clean, or new uniform, waistcoat as required.

The fact that Fred left his White Star buttons behind on his old waistcoat, when he left to join the *RMS Titanic*, seems to indicate the haste of his departure and his ability to pay for a new set, for the new ship. The *Titanic* held the promise of a more lucrative future for many of her crew, but that was well in the future.

Fred, like all the crew on the *Clyde*, also had to be prepared to pay a five shillings (25p) fine if he was caught using Company bedding, crockery or glass. The severity of this fine must be seen in comparison with the pay owing to him, at the end of his first voyage. It was just eleven shillings (55p). It was, however, usual for seamen with families to have an advance on their pay, before they set sail, to give their families some means of subsistence during the man's absence.

He continued on the long Brazil Mail trips on the *Clyde* until June 1904. During this time he progressed from Saloon Boy to Waiter. By then he also understood how the internal economy of the ship operated. The waiters, saloon staff and stewards were the ones at the passenger/crew interface and, therefore, they had the responsibility of driving the internal finances of the crew.

This was an era when 'class' was everything and passengers were expected to tip the crew at all times.[13] In this instance it would nearly always be the victualling staff in receipt of the money. In turn, a waiter or steward would pay the kitchen staff to ensure that *his* passengers' meals were always ready quickly and therefore, served hot. This was in the kitchen staff's interest, because it ensured the waiter received better tips. The kitchen staff in turn would pass some of the waiter's money to the scullions. So an internal monetary system existed on board which was driven by the skill and popularity of the stewards and waiters.

Sometime during this period Fred started singing to entertain the passengers, under the encouragement of Mr Bacon, the bandmaster. With his cleancut good looks Fred was popular with the passengers and this proved to be a good way of earning extra tips on the voyage. It was also an additional skill appreciated by both the ships' captains and the management - to have their own resident entertainer on board, at no extra cost, was quite a bonus.

During bad weather passengers tended to be on deck and understandably, ate and drank less than during a calm crossing,

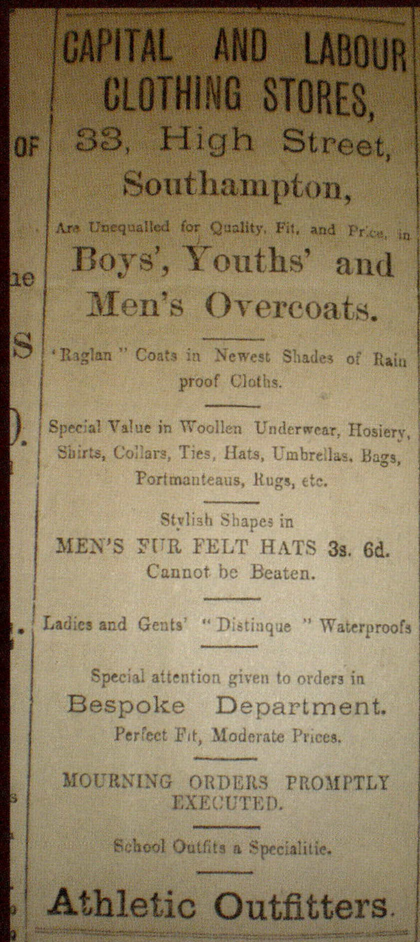

FIGURE 5.2

One of the many Capital and Labour advertisements that the company produced in the local newspapers.

(Courtesy Southern Daily Echo)

when they would be amusing themselves and calling on the stewards for snacks, or to run errands around the ship. Bad weather meant passengers made less use of the stewards, with a reduction in the tips they earned.

> Well my pet as the weather was so bad of course the passengers were not very often in and I am, as a good many others, out of pocket by the bad weather but still I dont mind all I want is to be at home where I should be, with the one who is my only real happiness and joy...

Initially this can be interpreted to mean that he has earned fewer tips, than he had hoped. However, that situation could not be taken as 'out of pocket', that is being in a minus situation at the end of the voyage. Perhaps he had still maintained some payments to the internal monetary system even when his own tips were reduced, thereby maintaining good relations with fellow crewmembers. With the closeness of the seafaring community in the town, and the constantly changing mixture of crew between ships, it would be to his advantage to have a good reputation with his colleagues on board.

By contrast a later letter gives some indication of how well he was tipped on a good crossing;

> I am very glad to be in New York after a very hard working passage out dont know whenever I worked so hard before and here we are in N.Y. before we know it, I am pleased to be able to send home 10 Dollars as it seems like the old times again, and I hope to bring £2.0.0 home with me as we are full up with 1st Class and I hope to go up there on the run home.[14]

Another letter refers to his passenger allocation, when he is given three first class passengers out of a total of nineteen, which is divided between thirty seven men, so he has been given 'a very good share', whilst on a previous trip he is 'given a very good table' and hopes that they will pay well.

Altogether the evidence suggests that Fred was a popular, hardworking and reliable member of the ship's crew, appreciated by passengers and management alike. It is not surprising that he had no problems signing on for a ship and there were few breaks in his service career, despite the fierce competition for positions.

Due to the unloading and reloading of the vessels in the overseas ports, the victualling crew were often obliged to take shore leave when they were abroad. As shown by the account of the orchid hunt in the West Indies, such trips were ideal opportunities for the release of youthful high spirits. Fred may have started to write of his experiences at sea as a therapeutic exercise - a result of the first incident he records - a riot in Buenos Aires. Starting as the 1904 May Day fiesta, it became a riot of some violence, during the course of which a shot was fired which hit a mounted policeman's horse. Fred's account continues;

> 'After this, all was a mass of confusion... men stabbing each other...children throwing stones at the police, while I and two more shipmates were simply spellbound...I did not know what to do, for all around was a shrieking, howling mass of people. Another shot was fired, this was from the Chief of Police and it was fired in the air, but as I afterwards learned, it was a signal. In less than a minute there were some 60-80 mounted police charging down upon the crowd, all of them with swords and pistolettes in their hands, I saw them hack their way through the howling mass!'

From this point Fred's account becomes somewhat disjointed; he appears to have been very shaken by the brutal attack and murder of one of the policemen, as he and his friends were fleeing for their ship and safety.

> 'Just as I was going by the corner of the football field, a terrible sight I saw, the victim of a most horrid murder, a poor foot policeman. There were about five men after him. One of them picked up a stone and threw it at him, hitting him under the right jaw. As it struck him, another one fired two shots at him. One hit him in the chest, the other in the head just over the left eye. This was not all. The same one that fired at him, ran up and took the policeman's sabre, using it to stab him in the chest and stomach and cut him across the face, severing his ear. He then did more, but it is too horrible to explain...I...heard a groan and looking saw a poor little boy about 9 year old, lying against the woodwork of the bridge with a shot right through the head. Oh dear that nearly sickened me. I went on not knowing where.'

The record of the riot was Fred's first effort at writing and it may well have been the need to confide in someone, or something, to unburden himself of this experience, which initiated the urge to write.

His next entry records the previous voyage of the *Clyde* in February and March 1904, during which they ran into heavy weather.

'We left Southampton on 12th March 1904, it was a dull day and as we got down Southampton Water we found it was going to be a bit rough.[15] After we left the Needles, we made for Cherbourg which is, in fair weather, a 6 hours' run, and leaving Southampton as we did, at 12 pm, we should have arrived there just before 7 pm. It was so rough crossing the Channel that we did not arrive there until 2 am on Saturday morning. The little 'dusting down' made us all wish we had not come away.[16] We left Cherbourg at 5 am. Saturday for Vigo, where we should have arrived at 8 pm Sunday. Having got outside Cherbourg breakwater we encountered a strong SW wind, with rough seas and as we got towards Ushant we got the full force of a SW gale. The old ship was just like a cork, we were being tossed about dreadfully. The seas came all over her. The ladies and children cried and everything was just one mass of confusion. The water was knee deep on her main deck, the cabins were flooded and that scared the women more than ever, whilst the cries of the children were heart-rending.

'Steward! Steward!' was what you heard all over the ship. You would go to where the cries came from and ask what you could do. They would ask you if the seas were going down and also ask you to stop and talk to them. Some poor wretches were dead sick, the look of agony on their faces told you what they wanted and that you could not give. 'I would give anything to get ashore'. 'Why ever did I leave my dear home?' 'What shall I do?' 'Oh, I feel as if I shall die'. Those were a few of the cries that you could hear. The weather did not get any better and we were beginning to think that the 'Clyde' had made her last voyage. We had sighted Ushant 12 pm on Sunday and for sixteen hours we couldn't pass it, because the seas and weather were so terrible. At times she would roll over and stay for 10 minutes before she righted herself. Those were the times when everyone's hearts were in their mouths, because a ship that rolls at 45 degrees is not worth much. It is a case then as to whether she goes right over or not and our old ship was rolling about 43 degrees and she scared the life out of everyone. Some of the crew were writing notes, as best they could and putting them in bottles. For three days we had this weather and then it abated a bit, as we got into the lee of the land. We arrived at Vigo 4 pm Wednesday, to the delight of the passengers who were almost frantic with joy and very soon found their way on shore for a while and a much needed change.

There were a few accidents. Our Captain was worst off, he was thrown right across the bridge and when he was picked up, it was found he had injured his back, shoulder and arm. One of the firemen was badly crushed down the stoke hole. The 4th officer slipped and broke his wrist and had to be sent home, as did the fireman.'

FIGURE 5.4

The waistcoat that Fred left behind, with his colleagues on the Oceanic*, when he joined the* Titanic.

FIGURE 5.5

Detail of the waistcoat buttons, showing the White Star burgee on the front and the name and place of the maker, Capital and Labour Southampton, on the back.

This particular voyage seems to have been 'jinxed' throughout and there is a temptation to think that Fred's imagination had run away with him. He tells of the Chief Engineer's sudden death; taking a prisoner on board from another ship, where he had killed the 'donkey man', and a lady, distraught with grief taking her husband's body back to Britain.[17] Fred relates how they were obliged to keep her locked in her cabin.

Altogether the whole story sounds most implausible and there is no surviving official ship's log to verify it. However, the crew list, meteorological records and press reports all confirm his account.[18] It seems that Fred's narrative can be trusted and therefore, it would be reasonable to accept his other reports as being truthful as well.

At sea, danger is never far away and over the years Fred grew to accept the various mishaps on board, as part of the job. Amongst the letters are references to a broken propeller, which infers he has experienced this before, or at least knew of the effects from other colleagues. A lightning strike, which hit the foremast causing the top to go overboard, he mentions in passing - failing to make any note of the fact that one of the large splinters caused by the break, narrowly missed Charles Lightoller, the *Oceanic's* Chief Officer. On another occasion he prophetically notes, there were large amounts of ice floating in the seaway.

Neither was Fred unfamiliar with the results of more extreme accidents at sea. The *Olympic* had suffered damage through a collision with the Royal Naval battleship *HMS Hawke*, but then returned to Liverpool safely for repairs under her own steam and he had seen the results of the *Suevic* incident for himself.

The *Suevic* had run aground just off the Lizard in 1907. Unable to refloat the ship, the decision was made to cut her in half, the bows remaining *in situ*, on the rocks. Meanwhile the larger stern section made its way safely to Southampton, under its own power and in reverse, aided by tugs. It was a considerable testimonial to the effectiveness of the watertight compartment system. A new set of bows was built by Harland and Wolf in Belfast, then towed to Southampton and the two halves successfully married up - a further testimonial to the skill of the shipbuilders. Fred would have heard the story and seen the *Suevic* in the dry dock, where she remained for many months, waiting for her new front section to arrive.

All these experiences, both personal and professional, probably had an influence on his reactions to the ultimate test in 1912. The account of the stormy voyage on the *Clyde* underlines his care and concern for the women and children in a dire situation and his own professionalism when dealing with them. There is no reason to believe that his approach would have been any different when faced with the need to evacuate the sinking *Titanic*.

CHAPTER 6

RUIN!

" The policeman at the door was apologetic.

"Mrs Lucraft?" he asked.

"Yes?" Martha Lucraft, answered cautiously. It was late evening and a call like this did not bode well. She could see chinks of light beginning to appear between the next door neighbours' curtains, as they started to peer out, curious about the loud knocking on her door.

"Hadn't he better come in, Mother?" asked Winifred from the kitchen doorway.

The constable came into the hallway and removed his helmet.

"Your husband is John Martin Lucraft?"

"Yes", Martha sighed, "What's happened now?"

"Oh, I didn't mean to alarm you, but we've got him in the cells. He was found in the gutter, in the village centre. Absolutely dead drunk. We managed to get him to give us your name and this address. We thought you might want to bail him out".

At this, Martha flared up.

"Bail him out! Are you out of your mind, or drunk as well? No, I most certainly do not, constable. Let him spend a night in the cells. It might help bring him to his senses."

The policeman left and returned to Totton police station.

It was April 1905 and the same old pattern had established itself again.

* * *

The Lucrafts' general store at Northam had been providing a modest but adequate income for the family. Martha was a good manager; Will, their son, had established himself as a ship's baker and was taken on by various ships on a regular basis; Eveline, their eldest daughter, worked in the shop and was officially 'walking out' with Will Mallett, who worked in an architect's office; Winifred, their youngest child, was working in a millinery shop in Southampton. Altogether, the family's finances should have been secure, but with Martha and Eveline running the shop, John Lucraft frequently found himself at a 'loose end'. What better way to while away the time, than the conviviality of the local hostelries?

By January 1905 it was apparent that things were not going well.

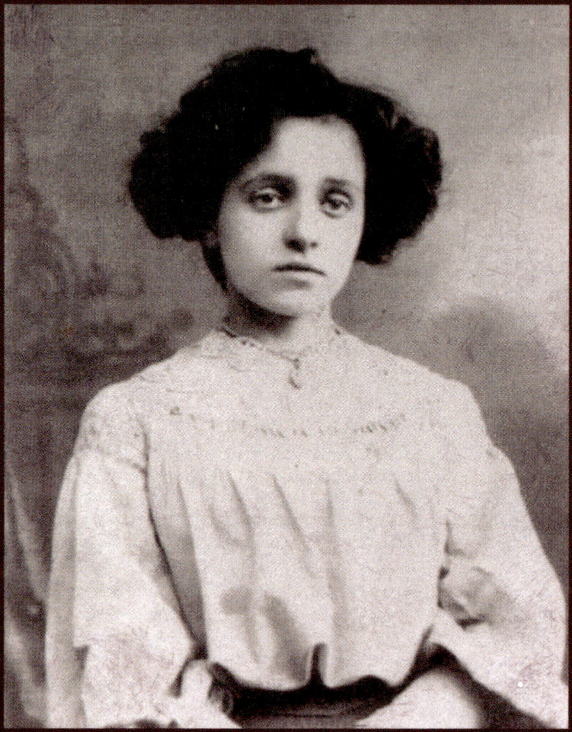

FIGURE 6.1

Winifred aged about sixteen, with her hair pinned up.

(Simmons archive)

FIGURE 6.2

The row of terrace houses where the Lucrafts first lived in York Road. The footpath across the strawberry fields went from here to Shirley Road.

Eveline and Will Mallett decided to avoid the inevitable embarrassment and got married in early February. They then moved into their own little home in Northam, rented from Eveline's new father-in-law. William Lucraft would also be untouched by the impending disaster being at sea as the drama unfolded, but Winifred still living at home, faced the full enormity of the situation. Only weeks after Eveline's wedding, *The Times*, on 18 March 1905, reported that John Martin Lucraft had been officially declared bankrupt. This time there was no safety net. His father was dead and his elderly mother and sisters were all in poor health. John Lucraft was ruined. The long term unemployment in the town was at its peak at this period and meant that the local community, which should have been sustaining the shop business, was not able to afford even the most basic of essential items. This coupled with John Lucraft's intemperate habits was bound to lead to financial disaster.

This was probably a period of great distress and trauma for Winifred. The family had always maintained a veneer of prosperity, as shown by the regular family portraits, but now they were leaving their home in disgrace for a different area, where they would not be known. The previous occasion, when they left Devon, would not have had such an impact on her personally, she was only thirteen then, but now at eighteen, she was painfully aware of the embarrassment and guilt of the situation.

It may even have been her and Martha's dressmaking skills, which fended off total destitution; working with their sewing needles to provide the necessities, as well as repaying some of John Lucraft's debts, so keeping them out of the workhouse, up the road. It was during this period that Fred Simmons was 'island hopping' in the West Indies, his last card to Winifred at the shop, was received in February 1905.

How different the comparison with his family must have seemed. Poor - yes, but hardworking, flexible and willing to make use of their skills in a variety of ways and *his* father's general store business seemed to thrive.

Both the Simmons family and their close relatives the Minns family, worked closely with the Docks exploiting any opportunities that arose. Work on the dockside as labourers, plumbers and fitters, seamen, painters, firemen, coal porters, carpenters, victuallers and stewards were all skills exploited by the family as various means of support. It is easy to imagine the happy-go-lucky supportive atmosphere of the individual comings and goings in Albert Road and in the family's second house around the corner in Paget Street; Thomas and Annie, Fred's parents, maintaining a central caring hub where children, new wives and husbands and grandchildren were absorbed and accepted without question. Name changes were common amongst their children - Albert became known as Roger and one of the girls

CADBURY'S CHOCOLATE
CADBURY'S CHOCOLATE
COOKE'S NEWS AGENCY.
WEEKLY DISPATCH
The paper with the most News.
EXPRESS
TRIBUNE
MIDNIGHT BALLOONING
MORE ARRESTS IN INDIA
FOUNDRY LANE
COOKE'S SERIES

became Minnie. These seem to have occurred simply because the individual preferred another name from their given baptismal one!

This period of her life may well have been the turning point in Winifred and Fred's relationship, as noted previously, there is a subtle change in the tone of Fred's letters at this time. It must have been very tempting for her to pour out all her worries and fears on paper, to this sympathetic and caring young man, who accepted the circumstances without question or criticism. How different from the tensions at home, with her own mother's strict attitudes to life and appearances.

No matter what Martha Lucraft's attitudes were, the family had to move and move quickly. Whether it was a traditional 'moonlight flit' with all their belongings piled on the horse and cart, to leave under cover of darkness, or a more decorous withdrawal during daylight hours, is not known, but the family went to Totton, moving into accommodation in Salisbury Road. What is certain is the need for the horse and cart to go with them; this would be their transport back and forth to Southampton.

With Eveline still living at Northam, transport was needed to keep in contact with her. The family's favoured route for the horse and cart was up through pleasant Regent's Park, trotting between the gates at the bottom and top of the carriageway, now Regent's Park Road. Going this way along Shirley Road, between the strawberry fields and orchards (a route Winifred would often walk in the future, to rendezvous with Fred), to Four Post Hill and then up Commercial Road, avoided the steeper hills in Millbrook Road and at Southampton West making it easier for the horse.[19] From Commercial Road the route would take them out to Six Dials and then along Northam Road and so to Eveline's little home.

Eveline and her husband had no such means of transport and so when they went to visit her family on Christmas Eve 1905, they walked the seven miles from Northam to Totton. However, Eveline was heavily pregnant. The result of her effort was that John Lucraft was dispatched off around Totton on Christmas Day to find a midwife but to no avail. Eveline's first child, Edith, was born at her parents' home in Totton, on Christmas Day 1905.

With the increasing closeness of Winifred and Fred, the relationship between her father and Fred also began to develop and it was probably due to encouragement by both Fred and his own son, William, that John Lucraft eventually decided to consider working on the ships. After all, he had considerable knowledge about provisioning and storage from the grocery trade. Surely this could be put to good use in the victualling department of a passenger ship?

Eventually he was persuaded and John Lucraft signed on with White Star as a waiter. Employment meant the family could afford to move again and they prepared to return to

Southampton in 1906. It may be that this change of career was exactly what was needed for John Lucraft. On board ship all alcohol was carefully accounted for and kept safely under lock and key, so ensuring that crew were not able to gain access during a voyage. At least while at sea he would have to remain sober.

Perhaps due to their travels through the Shirley area to visit Eveline, they elected to move to York Road in the Shirley/Freemantle area - a region known as 'Stewards Town' due to the large number of ships' stewards living there. No doubt Martha breathed a sigh of relief and considered the family to be 'respectable' once again.

CHAPTER 7

MARRIAGE

> 'Sorry I did not see you last night I was working till 9pm and have been in the Asturios (Asturias?) today and shall see you Sunday night at 7pm sharp at Four Post Hill. Mother sends her love and all are well at home'.

Time was always at a premium. Even between voyages Fred was working or involved with some activity working on other ships, probably helping to victual them before they sailed.

Throughout all his writing he is always very punctilious about times and dates (although the latter aren't always correct – for example he forgot that January should have been 1906, not 1905, on one occasion - a common mistake made by many people). This precision was no doubt learned through his work at sea; his day was strictly regimented by the clock, due to passengers' mealtimes and other requirements. Hence, it would not be unusual for him to expect Winifred to adhere to the same rules of punctuality. The fact that he gently chides her with the word 'sharp', suggests that her timekeeping may not have been all he could have wished.

To reach Four Post Hill from York Road, she would have used the footpath across the strawberry fields in Shirley (where some of the fruit was possibly intended for the passenger ships) and then, as they had done in the horse and cart, walked down Shirley Road through market gardens and the orchards of the Whitehedwood Estate, to her rendezvous.

Not for nothing was the phrase 'walking out' used for romantically involved young couples. Walking was the cheapest form of transport and conversation (or lack of it) was equally cheap as entertainment. Southampton had a variety of pleasant spots to roam; the Common, Parks and Pier being a few of them. Probably one of Fred and Winifred's favoured strolls, with its close proximity to the ships, would have been along the shore of Millbrook Bay and Point; before the 'New' Docks were built the sea came right up to the railway line. Longer excursions could take them to the outskirts of the New Forest, as sister Eveline had proved. This long distance friendship/courtship had continued for six years, when it was put to quite a severe test and no amount of walking would be able to keep them together.

FIGURE 7.1

Tiles commemorating the strawberry fields in the area.

FIGURE 7.2

The Royal Pier as Fred and Winifred would have known it.

(Author's collection)

* * *

One obvious feature of the letter archive is the lack of long letters before they were married. All the correspondence from this period is on postcards, or very brief and often formal messages on the ships' own greeting cards. What happened to those early letters? Surely they had to have existed; Fred was an enthusiastic writer, as witnessed by his 'diary'. Did Winifred not consider them of any importance at this stage? Did she destroy them to prevent them being found, possibly by Martha? Or did she keep them and they were found? The truth will never be known, but suddenly in 1908 Martha took Winifred to the tiny village of Woodchurch, in Kent. Here Martha was going to take care of her eldest daughter, Maud, who was home from China. Maud was expecting her second child and had her young daughter to care for as well.

When the twenty-two year old John Martin Lucraft married Martha, aged twenty-eight, in 1878 at Dartmouth, he also accepted responsibility for her daughter, Maud; who was the result of an illicit liaison Martha had had whilst in service at Killerton House, in Devon. However, Maud also spent long periods with her mother's relatives in Wales, where she came under the influence of the Welsh Church tradition. It is likely that the discipline of the Church, linked with her exposure to John Lucraft's intemperate habits, caused her to become a member of the Church Missionary Society initially and then ultimately undertake her role as a missionary in China. Here she married fellow missionary, Albert Seward, and now she had returned for a visit and to have her second child in England. Meanwhile Albert had remained in Shanghai, continuing with their duties there. Maud's children would therefore, have been Martha's first grandchildren, and Winifred's niece and nephew. Initially Martha stayed in Kent as well, but then she left Winifred to cope alone for several months.

At the same time Fred was still making the long six-week West Indies and New York mail runs. There was only about two weeks 'turn around' time between voyages, which meant he was often involved with setting up the ship as well. It was impossible to plan a trip to see Winifred, in Kent. Keeping in touch throughout this period must have been very difficult and Fred's card from Panama has a touch of near desperation about it:

> Dear W. Have not heard from you yet. Hope you are not ill, I am quite well and hope you are the same. Fred W.L.

FIGURE 7.3

Millbrook Shore and Point, where they probably walked and collected cockles for tea.

(Ayles Post Office, Testwood Road - Author's collection)

FIGURE 7.4

Further along Millbrook Road were the pretty Tanners Brook cottages and the open countryside.

(Ayles Post Office, Testwood Road - Author's collection)

Possibly Winifred was busy caring for the recently confined Maud, the new baby and the toddler. Keeping the washing up to date for all of them; towelling nappies, bed and baby linen, baby and toddler clothes, blouses, petticoats, drawers and bodices all needed to be kept clean and this probably without any running water. Moreover she was possibly sewing new clothes for the rapidly growing baby boy and the little girl. It is unlikely that Maud could have brought sufficient suitable garments from China, for either the children or herself. Winifred was probably unknowingly and single handedly, taking the place of the bevy of servants Maud was accustomed to have at her beck and call, in China.

The pressure on her own time is demonstrated by a postcard she had begun, addressed to her father, then a pantry steward on the *Majestic*, but never finished or sent. As well as time difficulties, there were the added complications associated with sending mail to Fred's ship at this period. Winifred was too far away to ensure her letters were taken on board by a suitable ship and must have had to rely entirely on the good auspices of the postal service to get mail onto a ship that would reach him, before his own vessel left a foreign port again. The alternative was to send mail either to her own or Fred's family and ask for someone to send it via a ship. Altogether it is hardly surprising that there were long gaps between her letters to him.

By autumn 1909 Winifred was back at York Road, in Shirley, but now the family had moved from Number 12 at the top end and were living at Number 23, half way down the road on the opposite side.

Fred was looking for a change in his lifestyle and in November, eventually decided to finish his seven-year association with the long distance Royal Mail Line ships. The White Star line had transferred the terminus of its trans-Atlantic New York crossing service to Southampton, from Liverpool in 1907, although a few ships still sailed from there as well. This service from Southampton went to Cherbourg and then on to New York, via Queenstown in Ireland. The liners were scheduled to make the return voyage in only three weeks. The relative brevity of the trips and regularity of the White Star schedule was attractive to local men looking for work as crewmen. Fred was no exception, but getting hired and becoming known within a new Company environment, was sure to take some time and effort. He needed to become a familiar face to the hiring officer, when new crews were taken on for each trip. Eventually he would be successful.

In the meantime he possibly found various types of casual employment linked to the Docks and the shipping, especially with all the various developments taking place to accommodate the larger ships of the White Star Company. So for a few months he was home and could spend more time with Winifred. Moreover it was Christmas and New Year. It is tempting to think of them, with a group of his siblings and their partners, celebrating the arrival of the New Year whilst the midnight clocks and ships' sirens greeted 1910. The result, in retrospect, seems inevitable; long separation, reunion and joyful celebrations. Winifred became pregnant.

To a large extent, it was an age of sexual ignorance for women and it is very possible that initially she was unaware of her condition. Women learned by experience what the signs were and how their bodies were likely to react to pregnancy. As already noted Eveline had been equally oblivious, despite her own size, that her baby's birth might be imminent and that it might not be advisable to undertake the seven-mile walk to Totton, for Christmas 1905. The effort obviously had precipitated the birth of her daughter, Edith.

Assuming that Winifred may have been unaware of her condition, it must have been Martha who became suspicious and probably put some very probing personal questions to her daughter. Her fears confirmed, it is hard to gauge what her reaction would have been. Would she maintain her reputation as a martinet or remember her own history and Maud's birth? We can only hope for Winifred's sake it was the latter.

Just when the situation became apparent and generally known is a matter for speculation, but Fred had now signed on with the *Oceanic* for the short three week return trips to New York. He stayed with the ship for the next two years, being generally regarded as a permanent crewmember.

Following his first three trips, Fred and Winifred were married at the Southampton Registrar's Office, at 4 College Terrace in London Road, on 28 June 1910. This was now a specially designated office for the Registrar, Mr Line; a more imposing building than the office in the High Street, where Fred's parents Thomas and Hannah, had been married in 1873. John Lucraft seems to have been at sea and so Martha is recorded as one of the witnesses. It also would seem logical, that with both her men folk often absent, Martha would have allowed Fred to move into York Road with herself and Winifred, but there is no direct evidence for such a move, at this time.

In the September Robert Ralph was born. Fred is overjoyed with his son and when baby Robbie is just a month old, sends him a postcard, from New York. Its picture and brief message reflect Fred's own quirky sense of humour and his quiet pride in being a father.

Hope you are quite well young man. Love from Dad xxxx

FIGURE 7.5

Fred's card to Robbie, expressing his pride in fatherhood and, as always concerns about health.

(Bamforth ©1910 Simmons archive)

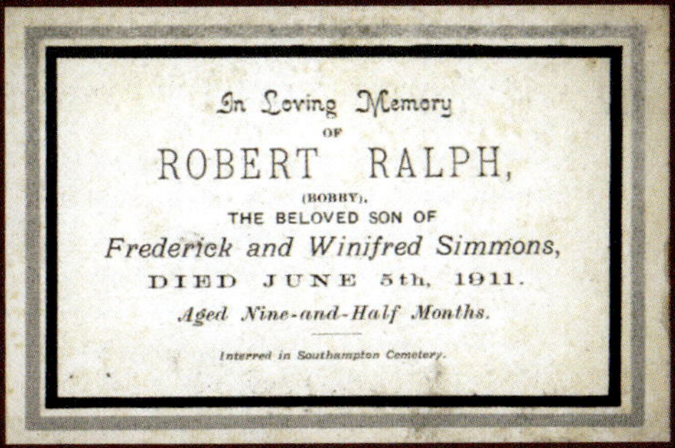

FIGURE 7.6 & 7.7

One of the memoriam cards printed after Robbie's death. These would be sent out to inform people about the death of the baby.

A letter sent from Queenstown, in Ireland, at the start of the same trip (many crewmen got into the habit of sending letters home from Queenstown on the New York runs) shows his concern for his young wife after the birth. Would 'they' - presumably her parents - hear her if she felt queer and called out in the night? But he sends her only positive news about himself - a disagreement has been resolved, he has a 'good table', the weather is fine and he is well. For the first time he uses his pet name for baby Robbie - 'Gig' - this would remain his nickname throughout his life.

* * *

Over the next few months life seems to have become a fairly regular routine. Fred enjoyed working on the *Oceanic*, saying it was a happy ship and he had quickly become established as a valued crew member.

FIGURE 7.8

Testwood Road, where several stewards lived, was directly behind Fred and Winifred's home in Millbrook Road. Mr Ayles, who had the postcards printed, is standing in the doorway of his corner shop and Post Office

By spring 1911, Winifred is pregnant again and is doing a little dressmaking to earn some extra money. Robbie is a happy baby apparently thriving and growing well. When he catches a mild summer cold there seems little need for undue concern. The cold develops into a respiratory infection, turns to pneumonia and on 5 June the unthinkable happens; Robbie dies.

They are both devastated, no doubt each blaming themselves for what was almost certain to happen in a pre-antibiotic era. No letter goes by without a reference to 'Giggee', 'our dear lost little boy', 'our ray of sunshine' and visits to his grave. The baby continues to be an important member of the family.

Ironically the day after the baby's death, on 6 June 1911, events were unfolding in the Docks which would cause them and many others, a period of uncertainty and stress.

FIGURE 7.9

A view of Southampton from the water, which shows in the distance on the far left, the area of semi-rural Millbrook along the shore of Millbrook Bay where Fred and Winifred were lived. In the distance, to the extreme right, are the outskirts of Newtown and industrial Northam, where they spent their teenage years. This was also the road that Fred would follow to join the Titanic on 10 April 1912.

(F.G.O. Stuart)

It all began with the coal porters. They had been told to report for work at 6am but were left until 11am to begin work. In this situation most ports paid 'stand-by money'; the Southampton employers did not. The coal porters asked for it and were refused; they went on strike, quickly followed by the firemen and seamen on the *Olympic*; all ports were drawn into the dispute and other grades of workers joined as well. The Corporation set up a conciliation committee and the employers agreed to the workers' demands. The dispute was settled within a fortnight, but it heralded a series of disputes throughout the coming months; some were resolved quickly, others took longer; some were official, some were not; some included other ports, some were in Southampton only. Ultimately the local unions developed a dispute with their headquarters and Southampton formed the breakaway British Union of Seafarers, which also accepted all the trades associated with the liners, including victualling crew members, like Fred. This immediately gave the new union over three thousand members and a much stronger negotiating base; by the Autumn the Docks had entered a much calmer phase of industrial relations.

The added uncertainty for work produced by these strikes, together with the usual need to sign on regularly, ensured that Fred never missed an opportunity for a trip, even when he would prefer to be at home. In late October he must now face Winifred's impending confinement whilst he is at sea. The prospect, after Robbie's death, fills him with anxiety. His next letter reflects his worries and indicates that Winifred was not feeling too well when he left. It also poses a bit of a conundrum - he seems to be staying at his parents' home in Albert Road. Possibly he was helping out there again, but there could be another explanation. This is the time when the birth was imminent, so perhaps he had been 'banished' from York Road. This was 'women's work' and mere men were not to be tolerated at such a time.

His next letter is from New York dated 1 November, still without news and by now he sounds quite frantic, but then he quite literally 'pulls himself together' and eventually says philosophically:

> ...but still when you dont know well you dont know and theres the end of it

Their second child was born two days later on 3 November 1911.

As so often happened, Fred was away for a family landmark or celebration and the baby's christening was no exception, he writes wistfully:

> Edward Reginald, will be his name today. I do so hope he will keep in good health
> he's a real dear little chap.

There is a clue that he was a 'hands on' father (he must have had plenty of experience with his younger siblings and young nieces and nephews) when he mentions 'his lordship spitting down my back'; presumably the result of 'burping the baby' after a feed. Fred's pride in his new son is apparent when he refers to him as 'a very forward young man' and asks Winifred to thank Teddy for lending him two shillings. The pride however, is always muted, by fears for the baby's health. The spectre of the unthinkable is ever present.

Early in 1912 a letter includes exhortations to Winifred to cheer up and keep trying for his sake. This is followed by a slightly ambiguous reference to 'things being better without the drink'. The inference would seem to be that Winifred was suffering from post natal depression - perhaps she had begun to indulge in a little too much stout (a popular tonic at the time) to aid her recovery, or perhaps Fred was referring to his own efforts at sobriety and how that improved relationships all round.

By February 1912 the living arrangements are becoming irksome and he is complaining that they hadn't had any opportunity to be alone together - there had always been someone else about. He declares this will all be different next time he is at home.

Although Fred is on the *Oceanic* at this point his promise may not be so easy to fulfill. The national coal miners' strike which had been threatened since early January 1912, was put into devastating effect on 22 February. Synchronised throughout the country every mine stopped producing coal on the same day. Stockpiles in factories sustained industry for a short while, but the stocks for trains and shipping were soon depleted. Road transport and haulage were still largely dependent on horsepower, but the great steamrollers and traction engines building the roads fell silent. Coal was the lifeblood of industry and without it the arteries and veins of the transport systems were useless. Southampton Docks was almost at a standstill; as liners arrived and were not 'coaled-up' so they lay idle at their berths. Some, like the *Oceanic*, did manage to continue for a short while by collecting fuel at other ports, for example many ships 'coaled-up' at Queenstown, when they called in *en route*, but after this trip the *Oceanic* would be idle as well; any coal remaining in her hold would be set aside for the *Titanic*. White Star Line were determined that *Titanic's* maiden voyage would go ahead on schedule and began to stockpile any remaining fuel from their other vessels, to ensure that their new liner sailed on time and with sufficient coal to complete her voyage.

Although the *Oceanic* was idle, Fred was not. He set about finding Winifred, Teddy and himself a home of their own. On 6 April they moved into their own house in Millbrook Road. Just ten minutes walk from Winifred's parents' home and behind the houses is Testwood Road, where several other stewards' families live.

It seemed a sensible move, support would still be on hand and the possibility of understanding neighbours would be reassuring, if they were needed. But most importantly, they would have their privacy and independence and be able to run their lives how they wanted, especially when the next baby arrived later that year. With Fred on the shorter New York runs he would be home more often and able to be more involved with everything.

They had weathered all the storms it seemed and now they could face the future with confidence.

CHAPTER 8

TITANIC

"Why haven't you signed on for the new ship?" demanded the White Star agent.

"I'm very happy where I am, sir," the young man replied.

"What's your present rating?"

"Second Class steward, sir,"

"I understand you entertain the passengers."

"Yes, sir. I sing a little."

"Hmm, well, suppose we send you up to First Class and look at the possibility of you doing a show for the passengers sometime?"

Fred considered the proposal. The extra money from tips would be useful, especially with all those rich people on board, some were even millionaires he'd heard - should be plenty of tips, especially if he did a show. Besides wouldn't it be a bit of one upmanship? His father-in-law, John Lucraft, had signed on with the *Olympic* again and his brother-in-law, Will Lucraft, was on the *Celtic* steaming up to Liverpool, before making the Atlantic crossing. Be a bit of a surprise for them when they returned, wouldn't it?

There was also the incentive of sailing with Captain E. J. Smith as Master - the cream of Southampton seamen sailed with him - this would be the only chance Fred would have to serve with such a legend and on a brand new ship, as well. The *Titanic's* maiden voyage was to be Captain Smith's last command, a suitable climax to his distinguished career.

On the other hand, Fred *really* did enjoy working on the *Oceanic*, it was a happy ship to be on, but for the present she had been cleared out of coal. It had all been transferred to the *Titanic* to ensure she could make her maiden voyage on time. Officially the coal strike, now entering a sixth week, was coming to an end, but it took time to get new coal mined and distributed to the coaling-up stations in the ports. Without any fuel the *Oceanic* could be delayed for some time.

"I'll just do this one trip," he finally agreed.

It would be interesting to compare the new ship with the *Oceanic*, the latter had been the Company flagship until now. Originally White Star Line had been owned by the Oceanic Steam Navigation Company, until it had been bought by the American International Mercantile

FIGURE 8.1

The journey of the Titanic's *anchor, from the factory of N. Hingley & Sons Ltd at Netherton, is a reminder that although this was the age of steam with trains and ships becoming ever more powerful, nonetheless the horse still ruled the roads. Even for the biggest loads, horses were the* and Marine Company in 1902. The first *Oceanic* was built in the mid 1800s as the Company's flagship and had been replaced by her successor in 1899. This new *Oceanic*, which Fred was associated with, had been seen as the pinnacle of nineteenth century shipbuilding for size, luxury and comfort, but she didn't have this new type of engine everyone was talking about. Certainly John Lucraft had been enthusiastic about the *Olympic's* stability, so this would be an opportunity to experience the same type of engine on the *Titanic* for himself.

And so, 6 April 1912, the same day the coal strike ended, Fred signed on at the company's hiring hall, as a First Class Steward, being entry 144 in the First Class register and giving his age as twenty-seven. There was no differentiation between the stewards' pay rates. They would all be paid three pounds fifteen shillings (£3.75p) for the trip but tips would improve on that rate.[20] Naturally Fred was sure that working in First Class would significantly increase his income from the trip. This was also the day that he and Winifred moved into 263, Millbrook Road. The expectation of a good trip and the prestige of working on the 'Big 'Un', apparently had encouraged the landlord to make the house immediately available to the young family.

The next day was Easter Sunday, spent with Winifred and Teddy in their new home and possibly including a visit to Robbie's grave in the early sunshine, to leave a posy of spring flowers there. It truly did seem like a time for a new beginning.

Fred had always been slightly cynical about the big ships. When he heard White Star were building another one even bigger than the *Titanic* (initially dubbed the *Gigantic*, by the press, but officially it was the *Britannic*) he remarked drily to Winifred,

"They're stretching the ships so much they'll have to call the next one the *Elastic*!"

a thought which may have been sparked off by the joke about the *Suevic* when she was undergoing her repairs. After her accident on the Lizard and her resulting bisection, she had been dubbed 'The Longest Ship in the World', as her bows were in Belfast and her stern was in Southampton.

With *Titanic* due to sail on 10 April, now began three busy days for Fred. New uniform was needed, he couldn't take his existing White Star waistcoat; new ship - *everything* had to be new. Apparently cabin arrangements would be different from those he was accustomed to; he would have a locker, so would not need his seaman's chest, this would be left behind as well. He left it, the old waistcoat inside, with colleagues from the *Oceanic* in readiness for his return to that ship. Everything, apart from their uniform, would be provided for the crew. He had no need to supply himself with eating utensils or crockery, there would be no more fines for breakages or for using Company china or linen.

One important item he would need was his music. An accompanist unfamiliar with Fred's repertoire and style would almost certainly ask for it. If he was to give a good performance and acquit himself well, he needed to have the music available. It appeared that the musicians on board would not be local, instead coming from other parts of the country - probably strangers to one another. The pianist's name, Mr Brailey, was unfamiliar to him, so he could only hope that they would work well, together.

His collection of popular light ballads had been amassed over the years and represented a considerable monetary investment. Each song with the accompanying piano part comprised, on average, four to six pages and had cost him between one and two shillings (5p - 10p) each. It was therefore, carefully maintained to be in usable condition. On this occasion, he found one piece which had fallen apart and the back page torn. He left it behind for Winifred to repair later. In the days before sticky tape, the best way for a repair, of this type, was to neatly stitch the pages together down the spine of the music. Using overstitch, this makes what is virtually a ring binding for the pages and enables the accompanist to open it out flat on his music stand. Winifred's even neat stitches were perfect for the job.

* * *

So Fred, together with others of his colleagues from the *Oceanic*, including the First Officer Mr Lightoller and seaman Fred Fleet, had been selected to join the prestigious new ship. White Star were looking for an experienced crew to take the *Titanic* on her maiden voyage. A large part of the crew for the *Titanic* were drawn from the two most luxurious ships in the White Star Line fleet: the *Olympic* and the *Oceanic*.

The Company could afford to hand pick the men and women they needed; the coal dispute was ending and there were plenty of people available, due to the many cancelled sailings, caused by the strike. But why should they employ crewmen who had not worked for several weeks and may not be as 'sharp' as the shipping line could have wished? It made sense to sign up people who had managed to continue working and despite the increasing fuel problems, the *Oceanic* continued to make her regular trans Atlantic crossings right up until the strike became official at the end of February. Fred's letter dated 2 February, was written on the last trip before she was laid up by the strike and berthed in Southampton Docks.

At the time of *Titanic's* departure the *Oceanic* and, with what was to be a touch of irony another of Fred's previous ships, the *New York*, were moored side by side in berths 38 and 39 at Test Quay. Both ships were facing downstream, with the *New York* on the outside, closer to the main channel. Neither ship was 'coaled-up' and so both rode high in the water, because they were lighter than they should have been. The *New York* was empty due to the strike, but the *Oceanic* remained empty so that all White Star coal could be given to the new ship. *Titanic* had steamed into Southampton just after midnight on 4 April, brought from Belfast under Captain Smith's command. This meant that his previous command the *Olympic* had left Southampton the day before, under the command of Captain Haddock, who had been transferred from the *Oceanic*.

* * *

Now began a period of frenetic activity on board. Everything was planned down to the last detail; the locations for glassware, china, silver and even the salad serving area in the dining saloon were all laid down in the ship's plans. New materials were still being delivered either from local suppliers or White Star; ashtrays, chopping boards, crockery, fruit and vegetables, glasses for the washstand fittings, inkstands, pads of Marconigram forms, pencils, playing cards, soap, stationery, the list seemed endless and everything had to be checked, before being put into its allocated place. The passenger saloons and cabins all had to be fully and correctly fitted out with the right class of equipment down to the last detail, so that even the standard of notepaper placed in each cabin was appropriate, for the class of passenger.

With all this last-minute activity taking place on the *Titanic* (it also included painters providing finishing touches to the paintwork) one longstanding local tradition had to be ignored. Normally it was the practice for a new, or refitted vessel, to be open for visitors, a day or two prior to sailing. On this occasion there were too many workmen still on board and fitting out still needed to be completed. Instead on Good Friday, the great ship was 'dressed over all' with her flags stretched above her funnels and reaching down to her bow and stern. The display was intended as a 'Thank You' to the people of Southampton, who had supplied most of her crew and many of the workmen now on board. Visitors to the Docks over the Easter weekend thronged the quayside and gazed up at the great bulkheads of the ship. Among the crowds on the Saturday, was the young curate from St Luke's parish at Newtown. He had watched the *Olympic*, sail in beautiful weather, at midday on 3 April. Now he brought his guests, the Master of Magdalene College at Cambridge and the Reverend Robert Quirk, to go over the *Kinfauns Castle* and to admire this latest achievement of the White Star Line, *Titanic*. The visit to the Docks gave them all, host and guests, a break from the intensity of emotion generated during the weekend when, so the curate reported, thousands in the parish 'raised their hearts in thankfulness' for the great celebration of Easter. Little did the young clergyman James, realise how significant the *Titanic* was to become for his St Luke's parish, little more than a week later.

FIGURE 8.2

Postcard of the Titanic *probably taken either during her sea trials, or on her voyage to Southampton. It shows how the design was amended to cover the promenade deck, unlike the open design of the* Olympic. *The card itself was also adapted, after the disaster, with the addition of the panel recording the loss of the ship.*

FIGURE 8.3

An artist's impression of the collision produced in the Lloyds Weekly News entitled; The Deathless Story of the Titanic. *It appears to be based on survivors' reports that there was a grinding, scraping noise along the length of the ship. Reports conflicted with one another about the strength of the impact, although one eyewitness, Mr Robert Daniel from Philadelphia, was recorded as saying that 'the whole front part of the steamer, it seemed, was torn away', before he jumped overboard.*

Meanwhile porters were bringing on advance luggage, which would not be needed on the voyage, to be stored in the hold. Later the cabin baggage would appear and have to be allocated to the correct cabins prior to the arrival of the passengers. As usual on the emigrant ships, the mix of passengers was extreme. They ranged from the very well off, to those emigrants paying just three pounds to travel in the bowels of the ship as third class (steerage) passengers, but nearly all hoping to make the crossing with a chance to start a new life in a new country. Fred was used to the international aspect of the passengers, all the White Star ships carried emigrants, including the *Oceanic* and *Olympic*, but on this occasion the differences seemed more marked, due to the number of millionaires on board, some of the richest people in the world travelling in the staterooms whilst the numbers of poor European emigrants seemed greater than usual.

When Fred was offered First Class status, it is doubtful his quarters would be allocated in the first class stewards' area - this was more likely to go to those stewards solely responsible for the stateroom passengers. The Upper Deck, where Fred's quarters were more plausibly situated, must have been the most eclectic gathering on board the ship, although the design of the ship did ensure almost complete segregation, between the different groups. But here, on the Upper Deck (E), the port side was taken up with crew's quarters, in particular the victualling staff including most of the First and Second Class stewards. Down the starboard side was a mixture of first, second and third class passenger cabins. Between the two, acting as an efficient barrier, were the boiler and engine casings, toilet blocks, drying room, barber's shop, elevators, stairways and bulkheads.[21]

So Fred would find himself one amongst many more stewards than he was accustomed to, and needing to prove his worth to Chief Steward Andrew Latimer, from the *Olympic*, if he wanted a good report of his time in First Class.

Eventually 10 April arrived, at 5.30am Fred left his home along Millbrook Road and started walking to Dock Gate 4 and Berth 44, where the *Titanic* lay waiting for her crew to muster on board, at 8am. He wanted to be early so his kit was stowed away safely before he and all the other victualling staff gathered; there wouldn't be any spare time afterwards. The muster and medical check for the crew was necessary to ensure there was a full ship's complement. It was not unusual for someone to sign on and then not come on board, for a trip. Different sections of the crew gathered at different parts of the ship to be checked off and any who did not attend by 9am were replaced, by standby crewmen, or by some of the many hopefuls waiting outside the Dock gate.

The *Olympic* had departed the previous week, leaving the way clear for her sister ship to take all the glory when she set out on her maiden voyage at midday. At last the waiting was over, the *Titanic* was cast off, with flags flying, the band playing and crowds on the quayside cheering and waving.

Before they sailed, the Docks had been rife with stories of bad omens and wives' premonitions, underlining the apprehension which many felt about the new ship; a fellow steward's White Star cap badge had broken when his wife tried to sew it on his cap, someone else told of having had bad dreams about the ship, yet another had deliberately left a treasured keepsake behind for this trip. Others were, in Fred's opinion, tempting fate by allowing their wives and children to watch the ship leave Southampton. Many, himself included, considered this bad luck and Winifred never came to see him sail. He had said his goodbyes to her and the sleeping Teddy, in their spartan little kitchen, before leaving. With a good trip, and this promised to be just that, they would be able to afford a few more homely touches in another three weeks.

At last, slowly, majestically the great ship began her journey and moved out into the channel past the many moored vessels along the quayside. Hurrying along the deck, with a tray of drinks, it seemed to Fred as if the silent, empty vessels were forming a guard of honour, in homage to the great liner. Then suddenly there was a ship in their path - the *New York*. As the *Titanic* began to pass the moored shipping, the suction caused by the great vessel in the water, drew the smaller unladen *New York* towards it with such force that its mooring lines were broken and suddenly it had swung out into the channel. Its stern was only feet away from the *Titanic*.

The cheering and waving on the quayside stopped and everyone, himself included, held their breath.

On the bridge, Captain Smith gave the order 'Full astern!'

The great ship shuddered to a halt and then slowly reversed its entire length, back towards the berth she had just left. Providence stepped in, in the shape of the tugs. They managed to get a line onto the loose *New York*, as she drifted towards Southampton Water and pulled her safely round the corner, out of the *Titanic's* path. Fears that the *Oceanic* might also break free, caused further delay as extra lines were fixed to her. At last, nearly an hour later, *Titanic* continued unhindered on her way. The near collision made Fred wonder momentarily about the omens, but he was too busy to ponder long.

He needed to learn his way around the ship. A steward could be called on by passengers in nearly all parts of the vessel, promenade decks, lounges, reading room, or smoking rooms;

he would need to know the quickest routes to fetch what they required and return to wherever they needed it. However, the majority of the crew were also involved in the learning process and once under way, a camaraderie soon began to develop between them. There were no 'old hands' on board to direct the new crew members. Those familiar with the *Olympic* had the advantage as, apart from a few minor changes the two ships were identical.

The first day at sea, crossing to Cherbourg, Fred spent helping to organise the stewards' department; checking and storing linen; cleaning and polishing silver, glassware and china, before replacing it in the designated cupboards and drawers of the ship; familiarising himself with the best route from his own quarters, along the central gangway known as 'Scotland Road,' up to the dining saloons on the deck above; checking the layout of the kitchens and the doors between the dining saloons and galley areas. All necessary information, if he and the other stewards and waiters weren't to crash into one another with their trays of food and drink. Like the staff in the luxury hotels of the period, the crew on the great ships were not supposed to be 'visible' to the passengers. Their routes around the liner should not, as far as possible, impinge onto the passengers' consciousness and never should the passengers catch any glimpses of the conditions in which the crew worked, behind the scenes. Everything should be perfect for the passengers and their every wish granted, with the minimum of delay. This was the way to earn the all important extra tips.

His daily routine would be very similar to that on the *Oceanic*, but on a larger scale. There was no denying the *Titanic* was very well appointed - no expense seemed to have been spared - every tiny detail had been checked; he had even seen Mr Andrews, the designer/builder himself, placing tables and chairs in their allocated positions. Overall, Fred was starting to approve of the ship and his misgivings, on having left the *Oceanic*, were beginning to be allayed, although he still found it strange to see the Blue Ensign fluttering at the stern, instead of the familiar Red Ensign. That however, was Captain Smith's choice and his right, as a Captain in the Royal Naval Reserve. He smiled as he remembered the story of the three coloured ensigns, one of the first things he had learnt on going to sea, to stress the importance of the Merchant Navy and its claim to be the rightful senior service, mainly to annoy any nearby Royal Navy sailors.

Before the death of Nelson, so the story went, the Royal Navy had had three sections when it went into battle and three separate Admirals - Admiral of the Red (acknowledged as the senior Commander), Admiral of the White and Admiral of the Blue. Nelson however, had a preference for the White Ensign even when he was in overall charge. After his death, when the roles of those at sea were separated into three different services: Merchant Navy, the Royal

Navy and the Royal Naval Reserve, the three ensigns were assigned - one to each service. The Royal Navy chose to adopt the White Ensign as a mark of respect to their national hero, the Red Ensign was then assigned to the Merchant Navy and the Royal Naval Reserve (RNR) took the Blue Ensign. Since then a Merchant Navy Master who was also a member of the RNR and had obtained a certificate of authority to do so, had the right to fly the Blue Ensign from his ship, if he so wished. It appeared that this was Captain Smith's chosen option for his prestigious last command.

During the crossing to France the crew began to learn more about the ship and how she felt when under way. The new style turbine engines certainly seemed to make her motion through the water more comfortable, there was less vibration than on the older White Star liners, which was pleasanter for both crew and passengers.

At Cherbourg some passengers left, while others from Paris joined, including some of the richest first class passengers; the Astors, the Duff-Gordons and the Rothschilds. More emigrants embarked as well, before they started the journey to Queenstown. Fred was beginning to feel more comfortable with the ship now, working conditions were better than he was used to on the *Oceanic*, and the stewards were 'shaking down' well together.

The biggest difficulty was the distance involved in moving about the ship and the large numbers of crew, nearly nine hundred of them altogether. The area where he was quartered, off the Scotland Road, was home to two hundred and sixty-five victualling staff, mainly stewards like himself. Another two hundred victualling staff were distributed around the ship - the largest section being about one hundred stewards housed in the Middle Deck (F) adjacent to the third class saloons. The stewardesses, maids and valets quarters were up on Shelter Deck (C) where only First Class cabins were situated and where they would be needed. The remainder; bakers, cooks, butchers, plate washers and kitchen scullions were housed in various corners of the ship, usually near where they would be working. Altogether the victualling staff numbered four hundred and ninety-four, making up 55% of the total crew.

Above Fred's quarters on E Deck there were one hundred and sixteen seamen and trimmers situated in the bow of the Upper Deck; in theory they had their own companionways, but there was still the potential for them to come down the Scotland Road, outside the stewards' quarters. No wonder it was the widest on the ship, to allow so many people access at all times of the day or night. He didn't know why it was called Scotland Road, but it was so busy it was much more like a road than a gangway.

The origin of the name for the crew's main thoroughfare, 'Scotland Road', may have come from a well-known cycle track through the Scottish Highlands. This was the era of the bicycle and crewmembers, weaving in and out and around each other, may have thought it was a similar experience to picking a route across a stony surface by bicycle. This suggestion seems to be corroborated by the name given to the Queen Mary's working gangway; the Burma Road, which was also the name of a cycle route in Scotland, long before the later connotation associated with the Second World War.[22]

In Ireland, Queenstown was busy, as always but the channel was too shallow for the ship to reach the jetty. Instead they moored two miles out and the tenders brought many more Irish emigrants on board, together with the port officials, reporters and more than thirteen hundred mail sacks. When the tenders returned to Queenstown, they took those passengers who were leaving the ship, the returning port officials and reporters together with the mailbags of mail intended for Ireland.

The ship was scheduled to be there for just two hours - he had to get a letter to Winnie. Grabbing a sheet of notepaper from one of the Second Class public rooms, he snatched a few moments to scrawl her a reassuring note and send it back with the returning mail on the tenders.[23]

* * *

The ship's routine had settled in nicely and the past three days had been pleasantly busy. The crossing was easy, the sea calm and the ship making good speed. When the coal strike ended White Star had lifted the speed restrictions on the *Olympic* and *Titanic*, so the great ship was going at near full speed.

An easy crossing always meant a busy time for the stewards. Passengers would spend more time inside amusing themselves, rather than out on deck, or languishing in their cabins. This trip was no exception and every night groups of passengers sat up talking, smoking, playing cards and expressing a variety of needs for the stewards to fulfil.

Sunday 14 April, a routine Sunday at sea. Captain Smith had held a morning service in the saloon, using the White Star prayer book's Order of Service; lunch had been served and passengers were relaxing, playing games, smoking or wrapping up against the cold, to stroll on deck.

Fred had heard there had been messages about ice in the area. No doubt that was the reason for the increasing cold which drove the passengers back inside towards the late afternoon. He thought back to some of the cold nights on the *Clyde*, when he had seen ice floes in the area. It had been so cold then that he had written to Winnie in pencil, for fear the ink would freeze on the pen nib. On deck now, it seemed very close to freezing, he was grateful the passengers had moved inside.

Once inside this gave them the opportunity for another pastime - sending messages home via the ship's wireless operators' connection to the Cape Race telegraph station on shore. Fred did not approve of this frivolous use of the wireless, he knew how important it was to keep in contact with other shipping in the vicinity. When the *Oceanic* had lost her mast in the lightning strike the previous year, they had been without a wireless aerial for over an hour, until they had fixed up a temporary one to get them to New York. During that hour the tension on board had been palpable. But then on that occasion, he considered, the weather had been very bad and the sea rough, whereas now, the sea was flat calm and it was a beautiful starlit evening, so there was probably no harm if they didn't have continuous wireless contact with other vessels.

The evening wore on. Ice floes could be seen floating past in the ship's lights. The sea was so calm that there were no ripples around them, until the wash, of the *Titanic's* wake, hit them.

Captain Smith went off duty and retired to his cabin about 9.30pm leaving Mr Lightoller on the bridge, until Mr Murdoch relieved him half an hour later. Just before 11pm Fred got to his own bunk, at last.

* * *

"Fred! Quick! Get up! General Alarm! We've hit an iceberg!"

He was being shaken awake by someone.

General Alarm - this was serious, no Captain gave that order unless the situation was perilous and the ship in grave danger. He was awake now and the other man was gone. An iceberg? Surely it couldn't have done much damage? The ship was so big...the watertight compartments...

Pulling his uniform on over his pyjamas, he hurried along Scotland Road and up to the saloon deck. It was just after midnight. In the wireless room the first distress call was being sent.

There was a sense of urgency, but no panic amongst the passengers, one even joked about being given an unnecessary lifejacket. There were more than three and a half thousand lifejackets stowed around the ship. The stewards' duty in an emergency was to rouse the passengers, get them into their lifejackets, allay their fears and help them to the lifeboats. Once there, the seamen and deck crew would be on hand to take over. As always, the stewards were at the interface between ship and passenger, the key point of contact for the transmission of information and general orders. They would be amongst the last to be allowed in the boats.

Despite his many years of experience at sea, Fred was not classified as a 'seaman' - he was, after all only a glorified waiter without any seamanship skills of value in a lifeboat situation. Like his comrades, he was expendable.

Nonetheless, training and professionalism both came into action and Fred returned below, to ensure the occupants of all the cabins on E deck were awake, dressed and making their way up to the boat deck. The command to load the lifeboats had already been given. He couldn't believe the speed at which everything was happening. Surely the ship shouldn't be tilting at such an angle? Hadn't the watertight compartments stopped the water coming in? Hadn't the *Suevic* proved how effective they were? And last year, after her accident, didn't the *Olympic* steam back to Belfast safely, because her watertight compartments had done their work successfully?

But there was no time to think about all that now, there were crying children and worried women to reassure and direct.

No parent should have to go through what he and Winnie had suffered when Robbie died. The children were of paramount importance. He picked a child up and took another's hand, whilst their mother briefly held her husband close, before turning away to follow Fred up to the boat deck.

The cold on deck was intense. Lumps of ice, he wondered if they were from the iceberg, slid down the tilting deck. He pointed out the 'pretty lights' of the flares to the older child, before putting them and their mother into the care of a seaman. They would be in a lifeboat shortly.

More women, more children, more lifejackets...he moved and worked automatically. This was his job. Two priests were near the rails, leading prayers and giving absolution to passengers, this was their job. The band was playing - good men, doing their job too. Down in the engine room the firemen continued working, providing the lights to help everyone else – good men doing their job as well.

He'd heard the second class passengers having a 'hymn sing' in their saloon earlier in the evening. They'd been singing the mariners' hymn *'Eternal Father'*. How often had he sung the words;

> 'Oh hear us when we cry to thee,
> For those in peril on the sea'

as a choirboy back home, in St Mary's Church? Too many times to remember now.

There only seemed to be men left on the deck now. Like himself, hanging on to some piece of structure as the incline of the ship steepened.

The boats were all gone. 'Every man for himself', the traditional last order on a sinking vessel, had been given.

He had a lifejacket. He was a good swimmer. It was a flat calm sea.

* * *

Five hundred miles to the west, on her homeward run to Southampton, the *Olympic* had tried to call her sister ship again, at 2.20 am. There was no response.

It fell to Captain Haddock, Fred's previous Master from the *Oceanic*, now Master of the *Olympic*, to relay the fateful news to the White Star office in New York:

> '*Carpathia* reached Titanic's position at daybreak. Found only boats and wreckage. *Titanic* had foundered about 2.20 am in 41.16 (*sic*) north, 50.14 west. All her boats accounted for. About 675 souls saved, crew and passengers, latterly nearly all women and children. Leyland Line SS *California* (*sic*) remaining and searching position of disaster. *Carpathia* returning to New York with survivors; please inform Cunard. Haddock'.

Captain Haddock, together with his crew must have felt a personal sense of loss, not only because this was their sister ship, but they would have known many of the crew as shipmates.

In the stewards' department, on the *Olympic*, John Lucraft thought, 'Thank God, Fred is on the *Oceanic*'.

CHAPTER 9

AFTERMATH

The letter lay on the doormat. Fred's first letter to Winifred in their first home. She picked it up and read it eagerly.

Titanic Queenstown 1912 - 11 April- postmarked 12 April 1912

Just a line in great haste to let you know I am feeling fine, and am rather pleased with the ship of course I dont know if I shall have a show or not but I hope to. How are you going on I hope you and baby are keeping very well. I expect I shall be comfortable here, when you write please address F.C.S. Simmons as there are 2 more of my name in the ship. Well darling I have no more to say now as I am in a hurry, love to all at home and heaps of it and kisses for you and Teddy,
from your ever loving husband

Fred

It was brief, even by Fred's standards, not even 'Dear W.' at the beginning, but it was reassuring. After all his qualms, he liked the ship, would probably do a show and was definitely relishing his First Class Steward status – F.C.S. Simmons indeed! How like him to turn his initials into a joke. Curious there were others with their surname on board, but probably not spelt exactly the same way. The letter told her everything she needed to know.

The *Titanic* was not scheduled to leave New York until the 20 April, there would just be time to get a letter to Fred by then, if she wrote within the next couple of days. Fred would be leaving America the same day that John Lucraft would be returning to Southampton on the *Olympic*.

It was a crisp April and Winifred spent the next two days arranging her new home, cleaning, washing and sewing her own and baby Teddy's clothes. At five months he was growing fast and she found some of Robbie's old clothes to mend for him. Nothing would be wasted; she would keep the clothes Teddy had outgrown, for the new baby in the autumn. The spring sunshine made the possibility of a walk to the cemetery on the Common, to visit Robbie's grave again, an attractive excursion. She arranged with Martha that they would walk with Teddy, in his pram, to the Common the next day – 15 April.

* * *

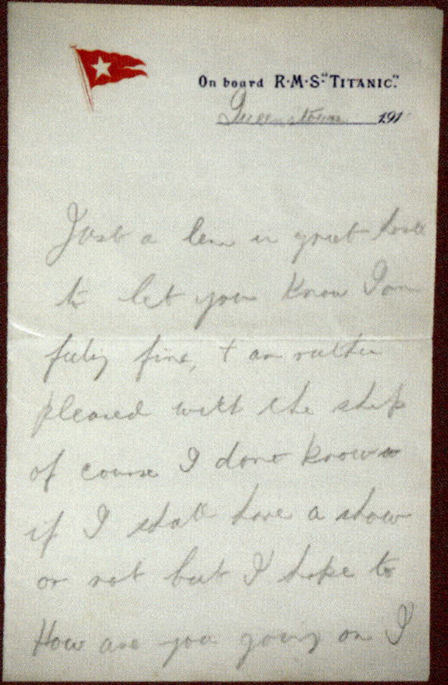

On board R·M·S "Titanic."
Queenstown 191

Just a line in great haste to let you know I am fairly fine, & am rather pleased with the ship of course I don't know if I shall have a show or not but I hope to How are you going on I

FIGURE 9.1

The letter sent by my grandfather, from Queenstown, to my grandmother, Winifred, reassuring her about the Titanic *and with his instructions for addressing her reply carefully, because there were two other Simmons crew members, on board.*

(Simmons archive).

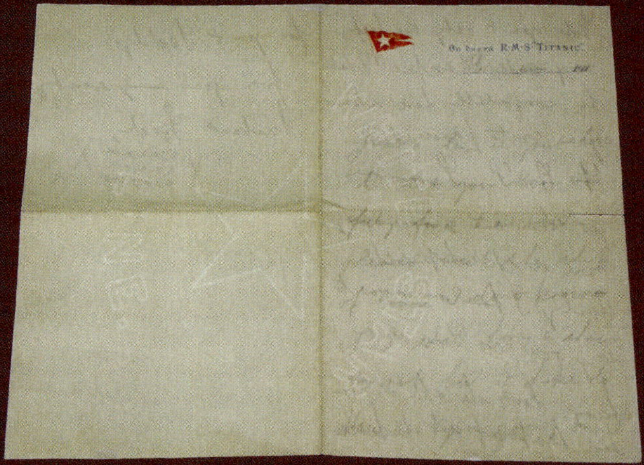

On board R·M·S "Titanic."

FIGURE 9.1a

Fred seems to have used stationery from the second class saloons, as some of his other letters from the Oceanic, are clearly written on the more expensive paper from First Class. Curiously it seems that only the cheaper grade paper had the White Star watermark, the more expensive stationery had the manufacturer's mark.

The morning was bright and clear, a good day for an outing. She had arranged to walk up to York Road to meet her mother, then together they would go to the Common, visit Bobbie's grave and then take Teddy to feed the ducks on the Cemetery Lake. A pleasant outing they would all enjoy. She got the pram out of the hallway, onto the front path. Humming softly to herself and Teddy, she tucked him in, he giggled and gurgled as she tickled him and she laughed back at him.

"I don't know what you're so happy about! Haven't you heard? The *Titanic's* gone down!"

The angry bitter voice of her neighbour cut into her cocooned world, bringing disbelief and horror.

And so the ordeal began.

* * *

Winifred, like all the other women, was dependent initially on the newspapers for information. They in turn were dependent on information cabled from America and that, relied on the information being sent by radio operators on a variety of ships at sea, in the area where *Titanic* foundered. Radio was still in its infancy and transmissions were often imperfect, with signals cutting across one another to become garbled, altering the original sense and even losing sections completely. These messages, when received by the White Star New York office, were then cabled to the Company's office in London. Hardly surprising then, that newspaper reports were contradictory, raising hopes and then dashing them; adding to the consternation and torment of the distraught waiting women.

Over the next twenty-four hours Winifred and all the other waiting women, were assailed with reports that the *Titanic* was either sailing to Halifax unaided, or was being towed there, that there was no loss of life, or that there was some loss of life. Eventually the stark truth, originally sent by Captain Haddock from the *Olympic*, reached the newstands. The *Titanic* had sunk; there were only about seven hundred survivors. Lists of survivors' names would be posted at White Star offices.

Survivors' names were being relayed to New York from the *Carpathia* via the American warship *Chester*, which had been dispatched to help by the American Government. Herbert Bride, the *Titanic's* surviving radio operator, who helped with transmissions from the *Carpathia*, was scathing about the American operator's competence, implying he was more hindrance than help.

The communities of crewmen's wives and mothers from Millbrook, Northam and Shirley began to gather together, supporting one another, hoping to glean extra information from each other or any other possible source. Nothing new, or definite, would be obtained from the newspapers; everything would have to be learned from the White Star offices in Canute Chambers, near the Docks. Among the waiting crowd of anxious family members was the little group of Winifred with baby Teddy, Martha and Annie (Fred's mother). Numbed disbelief and tension on every face in the crowd; the flags in the Docks and town flying at half mast; the pillars of the Audit House in the High Street draped in black crepe; the aspect of the town matched the sombre mood of the waiting women.[24]

The hastily scrawled lists of survivors' names appeared outside the White Star offices, posted on the railings there. Names were altered, corrected, amended or deleted as new information was received. Hopes were raised and then just as quickly, dashed again. Emotions in the silently waiting throng swung between relief and despair. 'SIMMONS' appeared at last. Thank the Lord. No, it is 'A. SIMMONS'. Perhaps the initial is wrong… but the hoped for alteration never came. Winifred remembered Fred's comment in his letter, 'there are two others of my name on board'. By the 17 April there were no more lists, no more corrections, no more hope. Fred was gone.

FIGURE 9.2

One of the memoriam cards that Winifred had printed to inform family and friends of Fred's death.

FIGURE 9.3

Lloyds Weekly News published this photograph of people waiting for news outside the Southampton White Star office. Winifred was to have her hopes raised and then dashed as the name 'A. Simmons' was written up, but the hoped for alteration to 'F. Simmons' never came. The duplication of names was an extra cruel twist to her ordeal. The poor quality is due to the cheap newsprint of the period.

MEMORIAL SERVICE

For those who have lost their lives in the S.S. "Titanic,"

At S. MARY'S CHURCH, . .

On SATURDAY, APRIL 20th,

AT 3 O'CLOCK.

ADMIT BEARER UP TO 2.50 P.M.

W. DURST, *Rector.*   A. I. RUSSELL, C. J. SHARP, } *Churchwardens.*

FIGURE 9.4

Winifred's invitation to the memorial service at St Mary's church.

With John Lucraft, on the *Olympic*, not expected home until the end of the week, Martha stayed with her distraught daughter, at Winifred's home in Millbrook Road.

The shock and tension of the last days took their toll and Winifred miscarried her unborn child. This was probably not an uncommon result for many of the pregnant women after the tension produced by the delay of definite news, followed by the shock of their unexpected widowhood and all the uncertainties that brought. In Winifred's case the early miscarriage was followed by a severe haemorrhage.

On 18 April she received an invitation to attend the memorial service at St Mary's Church, on the following Saturday, 20 April. This must have seemed quite callous at the time, when she had only received definite news the previous day. Moreover the invitation was only for one person, thus it would have denied her the support of her mother, during the service. As things were, she was too ill to attend, so missing an address given by the Bishop of Winchester to the congregation, which was probably relevant to every bereaved person present. In it he rightly touched on the power of imagining the fate of those destroyed by the disaster. He warned;

'It is a thing to darken the imagination, to turn the brain and crush the nerves. You must not feed yourselves with horrors, but look up and come away'.[25]

But Winifred was not there to hear the warnings, even so it seems unlikely that she could or would have been able to heed them. Her thoughts seemed to be constantly concerned with the ship's sinking and Fred's possible end. Did he get trapped in the ship somewhere watching the water coming towards him; the cold of the water must have been intense, the pain of it creeping into his body, his bones, his mind; struggling in the water, trying to find a lifeboat, getting weaker, crying out to someone, anyone, for help. What if he'd been floating unconscious in the water when the *Carpathia* came? He could have survived if the *Carpathia* had picked him up, but it did not.[26] Worst of all was the thought Fred had been safe but alone, on a piece of wreckage, unseen by the *Carpathia*, watching her steam away and knowing all hope was gone. Such thoughts were fruitless and only underlined her own state of mind, hindering her recovery from the miscarriage. She began to slide into depression.

The *Olympic* was running behind schedule, due to the deviation in her return route in her attempt to assist her sister ship. She didn't arrive in Southampton, until the early hours of 21 April and she arrived with £2,000 collected from the passengers and crew, for those affected by the loss of the *Titanic*. The money was passed over to the town's mayor, Alderman Bowyer, so beginning the fund for the dependants of those lost in the disaster.[27]

Olympic's return also brought John Lucraft home to find a very different family situation from the one he had left behind, less than three weeks previously. His own home was abandoned, his wife was caring for his grandson and desperately ill daughter, whilst his son-in-law was dead.

Martha, ever practical, must have realised there were going to be financial difficulties ahead. Winifred was too ill to move back to York Road; John Lucraft's earnings wouldn't pay the rent for two homes and the extra money for Winifred and Teddy's keep. Consequently Martha and John Lucraft moved into 263, Millbrook Road with their daughter and grandson – it was the most sensible course of action, with the baby to care for as well. Winifred was too ill to cope with his needs alone.

With her daughter needing almost constant care, Martha hired a girl as Teddy's 'nursemaid'. She would take him out in his pram every day, to give him some fresh air and remove him from the increasingly oppressive atmosphere in the house. The girl was careless. One day she returned shortly after having left the house, the pram was scratched and dented, Teddy bruised, cut and crying. She had upset the pram and the baby had been catapulted out. The girl was dismissed on the spot.

Now, Martha had two very sick people in her care. It must be taken as an indication of her practical approach and great strength of character, that during this period she did nurse both Winifred and Teddy back to health. It was a long, slow process. She was coping alone with medical conditions only vaguely known and understood at the time. Winifred was not only suffering from depression, but the miscarriage and haemorrhage had left her anaemic, whilst Teddy unknown to anyone, had suffered kidney damage in the fall from the pram.[28]

* * *

Meanwhile out in the Atlantic, the task of collecting bodies was undertaken by the two cable laying steamers, *Mackay-Bennett* and *Minia*. Searches continued into early May, with two fisheries vessels the *Montmaigny* and *Algerine* being commissioned by White Star until 8 June, when the *Algerine* returned to St John's in Newfoundland with the single body they had recovered – saloon steward James McGrady. There were no more official searches after this. Halifax in Nova Scotia, received the bodies and held them for identification, ultimately taking on the responsibility of one hundred and fifty graves held in the Fairview Lawn Cemetery, the Baron Hirsch Hebrew Cemetery and the Catholic Mount Olivet Cemetery.

Mrs Wormald living in Testwood Road, almost directly behind Winifred, had received notification that her husband, another first class steward who would have been working alongside Fred, would be buried at Halifax early in May. Still suffering from shock several weeks later, she bought steerage tickets for herself and six children on an emigration vessel to New York, apparently intending to visit her husband's grave, but not realising the distance and travel involved to reach Halifax, from New York.

On their arrival, the American authorities decreed that as she had no visible means of support the family should be shipped straight back to Southampton. During the return voyage fellow passengers, touched by her story, made a collection of forty pounds for her and the children. This was more useful than they realised at the time of the donation. When the Wormalds returned to Testwood Road they were to find they had been evicted due to non-payment of rent. Sympathetic neighbours had taken the family's furniture and stored it in their own homes and garden sheds, awaiting the Wormalds' return. With the money from the passengers, the family was able to rent another property nearby, and later they were supported by the Titanic Fund.

Perhaps it was the knowledge that her husband, an Anglican, had been buried in the Hebrew Cemetery at Halifax which prompted Mrs Wormald's rash journey. Maybe it was her intention to get him moved to the Fairlawn Cemetery, by visiting the undertakers and White Star agent in Halifax. Whatever her motives or intentions, his body remains in the Baron De Hirsch Cemetery, adjacent to the Fairlawn site. His name, together with his colleague, Fred Simmons, can be seen on the memorial plaque in their own Parish Church of Holy Trinity, at Millbrook in Southampton.

At least Winifred did not face complete destitution and had her family to give support through the difficult months ahead. Fred's body was never recovered, which meant she was also spared the trauma of receiving a letter similar to the one probably received by Mrs Wormald, in which White Star stated:

> We regret that we do not see our way to bring home the bodies of those recovered free of expense, and in cases where this is desired to be done it can only be carried out provided the body was in a fit state to be returned and upon receiving a deposit of £20 on account of the expenses.
>
> The remains of those not returned to England we are arranging to have buried at Halifax, each in a separate grave, with a suitable headstone and we hope this latter arrangement will commend itself to you.
>
> While the Line cannot be held responsible for the results of the unfortunate accident we will willingly bring your case before the Committee of the Relief Fund.

Such sentiments must have caused distress in many Southampton homes, especially as the Company had announced originally that the bodies of passengers and crew would be transported free of charge. Compared with the wages paid to the crew, the charge to transport the bodies home was equivalent to at least five months' salary. So what had prompted this cruel change of heart with a charge that was completely outside the means of the families ?

The White Star Line has suffered much criticism, both at the time of the disaster and during the intervening years. Some of it was undoubtedly deserved, but some of their actions perhaps need a brief reappraisal, within the context of the period.

The one over-riding criticism which cannot be escaped was the lack of lifeboats, especially when the ship's original designer, Alexander Carlisle of Harland and Wolff, had recommended sixty-four lifeboats to ensure everyone on board would have a place, if necessary. He was dismissed and the Company stuck to the inadequate regulations from the Board of Trade; regulations which stipulated the maximum number of lifeboats as sixteen, a figure that had not been updated since 1894, when the idea of ships the size and capability of *Titanic* had never seemed possible. In addition the ship was fitted with four Englehardt 'collapsible' lifeboats, making a total of twenty altogether. It has to be noted, however, that there were sufficient lifejackets on board for everyone, both passengers and crew. Nonetheless,

the Company was seen, by the public, to be the problem. The reduction in the number of lifeboats to the legal level was perceived as a cost-cutting exercise, as was the lowered height of the watertight compartment walls.

Perhaps White Star's greatest mistake was to believe naively their own rhetoric about the ship; as the Bishop said in the address at St Mary's Church, 'the *Titanic* will stand for a monument of warning to human presumption'. It may be that the greatest presumption of all was that size could be equated with 'safety'. It clearly could not, and the foundering of the ship seems to have caused the Company to go into something best described as 'Corporate Shock'. By their own admission there was a delay between the receipt of the message from Captain Haddock, on the *Olympic*, confirming the total loss of the *Titanic* and relaying that news to the waiting press. Not a long delay, only approximately thirty minutes, but surely indicative of the total disbelief, which each member of the Board, felt at the news. Their faith in the ship designers and builders was shaken to the core and the shock seemed to put them in a 'state of denial', producing an inability to cope with either the families of those lost, *or* the crew members who survived. However, their actions, from the time they received the news, have to be seen within the context of the period and the prevailing social attitudes.

'Life' and workforces were still relatively 'cheap' and so manpower resources could be easily replenished or replaced. For the poorer members of society life was full of risk, hazards at home and at work, accidents causing incapacity, and ill health from a variety of diseases virtually unknown today. Diphtheria, scarlet fever, smallpox and tuberculosis were all too common at that period and any one of these could leave the sufferer permanently incapacitated. As shown by Fred's letters home, health and the ability to support oneself and family was an over-riding concern. Therefore, within such a harsh context, White Star had little need to show undue concern at the loss of crewmen – accidents frequently happened and manpower was easily replaced, by others needing work. Merchant seamen had always operated within an open market and this would still continue, ensuring the usual supply of the manpower needed, for vessels. What does seem to have been a greater problem were those that survived; they remained as a reminder and embarrassment to the Company.

The greatest reminder of the tragedy was the survival of the Chairman, Bruce Ismay. Controversy followed him for the rest of his life and rumour piled upon rumour about how he gained a place in the lifeboats and that his presence on the Board was an embarrassment and that he should resign. The facts were slightly different. Ismay had already given notice that he wanted to relinquish the Chairmanship of the Company and his journey to New York, on the *Titanic*, was intended to make the final arrangements for the handover to his successor.

He left the Company as he had planned, but the ongoing controversy caused him to slide into anonymity.[29] The same fate seems to have been shared by a number of crewmen who survived – none of those who remained with the Company gained promotion, others changed allegiance and joined other shipping lines, whilst another group left the sea shortly afterwards. In later years many would claim that their presence seemed to be an embarrassment to White Star, with which the Company seemed unable to cope.

Also, within the context of easily replaceable labour, it was standard practice for all shipping lines to stop the crew's pay when a ship was wrecked or sunk. Once again therefore, White Star was only following accepted procedures, by not paying for work not received, because a voyage had not been completed. In a free labour market, it was not unusual for crewmen to desert at various ports, or just not report for duty at the start of a voyage, as shown by *Titanic's* own manifest and Fred's previous records. Hence, shipping lines did not pay wages for a 'voyage not completed' (as appeared in the crewman's discharge book) a phrase which included shipwreck. Thus, White Star Line was only acting within the accepted procedures of the period and the accusations of callousness should be considered as unjustified, within the context of the time and accepted procedures.

Other criticisms against the Company were caused by their terminology to crewmen's families using such phrases as 'your missing husband', or 'your supposed drowned son'. Viewed objectively however, without an identifiable body as definite proof of death, what other terminology was possible?

Similar criticisms have been made that they were slow passing information to the Coroner's Office, for the issue of death certificates to the families. The opposite appears to be more accurate. White Star had made payments to the surviving crew members by the end of April, for their four and a half days service on the ship and all the surviving discharge books were rubber-stamped with the traditional phrase, 'voyage not completed'. As usual, all responsibility to these surviving crewmen was now at an end, unless they signed on to another White Star Line ship. The Company office then drew up a complete list of the crew, recording all those 'supposed drowned' and those 'survived' by 14 May 1912. A copy of this list was then passed to the Board of Trade Registrar's Office for their own records, by mid-June. Here however, it became mislaid and at the end of October the Registrar General's Office was requesting a duplicate list direct from White Star Line. Understandably, the Registrar was being pressed for 'many urgent applications for certificates of death, but these cannot be dealt with until the lists of crew and passengers are completed', only then did the loss at the Board of Trade become apparent. It must also be remembered that all these lists, including copies,

FIGURE 9.6

A newspaper cutting of the little wooden St John's church, at Fairview cemetery, Halifax. Winifred kept it with Fred's letters.

were written by hand – the age of the fax and photocopier was still to come. The lists required must have seemed endless to the clerks; a complete alphabetical list of everyone on board including both passengers and crew; separate lists for passengers, sorted into first second and third class; lists of all those who survived; lists for all those lost and a list of amendments to all the other lists. It was a huge undertaking, which had to be done manually by the office staff, within a relatively short timescale.

For the White Star office staff at New York, London and Southampton the first weeks after the tragedy must have seemed unreal. All the initial lists produced were needed now for other tasks; calculating the proportional amounts of money owed to all the crew (whether 'survived' or 'supposed drowned'); reporting to the official enquiries; attending the many memorial services; coping with the press and replying to dozens of letters from all over the world. It was a monumental task and one for which they had not been trained. Perhaps, in retrospect, it is not surprising that some things were not done as well as they should have been. The letter to the bereaved families about the shipment of their relatives' remains was possibly the most extreme example of their inexperience when dealing with a catastrophe of such magnitude.

For the White Star Agent, P.A.S. Franklin, in Halifax, the task was probably easier. Here there was objectivity, the people were unknown to him; there is equality in death – all corpses are alike – this was a practical task, which just needed to be properly organised. Arrangements were made with various vessels to search for and collect the bodies from the wreckage area; undertakers were commandeered and dispatched in the *Mackay-Bennett* and *Minia*. The bodies were all to be embalmed and placed in coffins. Canvas bags were provided for those who would be buried at sea. In the event, the ships ran out of both coffins and canvas bags, which meant that some bodies were brought ashore at Halifax, only covered by sheets. This was used as further criticism of White Star by poorly informed individuals who inferred the Company had insisted on the maintenance of class distinctions, thus first class passengers were to have coffins, all other passengers being given canvas bags and the crew members had nothing but the sheets to cover them. Logically such an idea is senseless, as most of the bodies remained unidentified, thus no class distinction could safely be made, so all were treated with equal respect. The White Star agent even bought suitable clothes, for the burial of many victims and ensured that each of the recovery vessels had a priest on board, to officiate for the burials at sea.[30]

The Company's reasons for apparently reversing the original plan to ship bodies home free of charge, to wherever the relatives requested, seem more difficult to understand, but a number of factors may have come into consideration, either consciously or unconsciously. The suggested charge of twenty pounds as given in the standard letter to relatives, made it almost certain that no crewmen's bodies would be shipped home. This proved to be the case, with only one crewman's body being returned to the U.K. There was also the viewpoint that those who had worked and perished together, should also remain together in death. Lastly, in White Star's shocked state, there may have been the unconscious thought that a large number of *Titanic* victims in one place, mainly Southampton, in the U.K. would be a continual reminder to the public of the tragedy. Their burial in a small town, almost a backwater, in far off Nova Scotia must have seemed preferable – eventually the graves and the disaster would be forgotten. Instead the reverse has proved to be true; Halifax has grown and now surrounds the graveyards which in 1912 had been well outside the town, and thousands of visitors from all over the world, make the pilgrimage to visit the graves every year.

* * *

But for the women of Southampton, boardroom discussions, burial arrangements and Registrar's lost documents were all unknown, far removed factors. They only knew that there were long delays and little help available. Winifred, like the other women, received the balance of the wages owed to Fred in May 1912 – it was just fifteen shillings (75p). Apart from that she was left to her own resources. There was talk of a fund for victims' dependants but she, like all the others affected by the disaster, needed a death certificate in order to make a claim to the nascent Relief Fund. It was several months before the certificate eventually arrived and only then could Winifred, together with the other widows and dependant relatives, apply to the Mansion House Fund as it was known initially, later it simply became known as the Titanic Fund.

CHAPTER 10

ST LUKE'S

The young man alighted from the train at Southampton West railway station. A large figure, looming by the side of the ticket collector, moved forward with outstretched hand,

'Welcome to Southampton and St Luke's, James',

'Thank you, Doctor Trevaskis'.

They left the station and walked in thoughtful silence, towards St Luke's vicarage on the Avenue. The silence was broken only once, when the Doctor suddenly remarked in slow and measured tones,

'Southampton lies in the second degree of rainfall'.

Feeling unable to question his potential employer, James remained mystified for the rest of his life, about the meaning of this pronouncement.

It was the middle of July 1910 and the young man, had come to seek the curacy of St Luke's parish in the Newtown area of Southampton (*See map on page xi*). The parish was situated between the Avenue and the industrialised Northam area of the town. On the eastern side of the parish was the railway line and the engine sheds, together these made an effective barrier between Newtown and Northam, as there was no bridge over the line.

Newtown had grown up when the large estates surrounding Bevis Mount, Portswood House and Westwood House had been broken up and sold for building purposes. Bevois Valley Road, was the main thoroughfare of the parish; stretching from Onslow Road at the Avenue end, through to Lawn Road at Portswood, it formed the backbone for all the other streets. Along its length it not only housed a large number of the parishioners, but also catered for most of their needs. There was a selection of shops comprising bakers, beer retailers, butchers, greengrocers, grocers, three public houses, a coffee shop, furniture shop, tailor and, probably reflecting the needs of the community more starkly than anything else, the large double fronted second hand shop and the equally large pawnbroker's shop. Originally many of the Newtown houses had been built for the artisan population and had an average of five or six rooms. Now, however, they were increasingly occupied by greater numbers of the working-class population comprising large extended families. To accommodate the extra people some houses were subdivided into smaller accommodation units.

FIGURE 10.1

The Reverend Beaumont James, curate of St Luke's, who coped with the bereaved families of the Titanic *disaster in the parish.*

(James Family Archive).

Despite the overcrowding in some houses it is apparent that infant survival rates in the area were not bad. The numbers of children recorded as having died in each family, a statistic collected by the 1911 census returns, were much less than the average recorded in the worst areas of the town, including the Docks where the Simmons family had raised their children. Here the expected death rate, in 1890, for children under five years was forty-two percent.[31] It is likely that the larger, airier rooms in the Newtown houses were one of several contributory factors increasing the children's survival chances.

It was during this period of expansion and new building, during the 1850s, that St Luke's church itself had been built. Originally the site had been occupied by a Wesleyan Chapel which was converted to a church in 1850. However, the first incumbent in 1850, Reverend Frederick Russell, was such an impressive preacher and drew such large crowds that the need for a bigger church was evident within the first year. The lord of the manor of Newtown, Thomas Chamberlayne, from Cranbury Park at Otterbourne, gave the land and with further monetary gifts the new church was built. Fifty years after Russell, Dr Trevaskis was an equally impressive preacher and St Luke's was usually full to capacity, when he spoke.

An earlier gift of land had enabled a school to be built in1847, but this had become redundant with the advent of the new Bevois Town School Board schools in the 1870s. Dr Trevaskis, however, retained the old school buildings for the use of the parish. It seems likely that this was where the Sunday School was based and where Bible classes were held. As well as the church, the parish also contained the South Hants Infirmary which was intended to provide medical and surgical aid to the poor and infirm of the southern part of the county.[32]

This, then, was the church and parish where Beaumont James arrived, to take up the first position of his ministry. After his initial visit in July, five months later on 31 December 1910 fresh from his ordination, he returned as curate to the vicar of St Luke's. He received an annual stipend of one hundred and forty pounds; an amount that meant he was paid little more than many of his parishioners.

Dr Trevaskis believed that 'the best way to learn to swim is by drowning' and so his curate was catapulted straight into church and parish life. The first day of the New Year, being a Sunday, James assisted at five services and took a Bible Class of lively youths. On the second of January he took his first funeral, remarking that 'the mourners did not seem deeply grieved' and admitted that this was the real beginning of his education. The comment about the mourners should perhaps be taken as reflecting the conditions within the parish, where sickness was rife and fatal accidents were not uncommon. Apparent lack of grief was not indifference to loss, but the familiarity of death within the community and its acceptance as a part of existence.

By Easter 1912, James had 'learnt to swim' and was a familiar figure around the parish visiting sick churchgoers and non-churchgoers alike; taking the Bible Classes; training Sunday School teachers; running Confirmation classes; organising the choir; maintaining links with other clergy; making hospital visits; holding occasional services in the Royal South Hants Hospital Chapel and supporting the parish football and cricket teams. So it is not surprising that people readily turned towards him, when tragedy struck the parish.

Easter being the most important date in the Church calendar, guest clergy were sometimes invited to lead the services over that weekend. This year James, with the approval of Dr Trevaskis invited two such guests, from his Cambridge University days, to officiate at the St Luke's three-hour liturgy on Good Friday and to participate in the joyful Easter Day services, 'when thousands raised their hearts in thankfulness'.[33] Therefore, on the Thursday evening, James met the Master of Magdalene, the Reverend Stuart Donaldson and the Reverend Robert Quirk, scholar of King's Cambridge and a friend from their days together at Guildford, who was teaching at Winchester College. The three men all returned to James's lodging in Denzil Avenue, not far from St Luke's church. On the Saturday, the curate took his guests to visit the Docks where they went over the *Kinfauns Castle* and saw the *Titanic*, before they caught the eleven o'clock boat to the Isle of Wight and went to visit Carisbrooke Castle.

On Easter Monday his guests departed in the morning, and James took himself on a short holiday; a traditional time for many clergy to take their holidays. After cycling to Romsey, where he stayed for a few days, he continued by bicycle and train to Banbury to visit his mother and then on to London, to see a parishioner in the Fulham cancer hospital, before returning to Southampton on the evening of Friday 19 April. Immediately he found himself at the heart of the *Titanic* tragedy.

As soon as he returned to St Luke's Dr Trevaskis called James to the Vicarage, to discuss possible memorial service(s) for the victims of the tragedy. A service at St Mary's, the Seamen's Church, had already been arranged for the following afternoon, Saturday 20 April. Some of their own parishioners would have received invitations to attend this, as had Winifred. Not all mourners from St Lukes's would wish to go to St Mary's, while others may have been unable to travel. They needed to consider something suitable for St Luke's.

As a result of that evening meeting, James found himself supporting not only bereaved and sometimes near destitute parishioners, but Dr Trevaskis as well. The vicar's wife was terminally ill and had been in considerable pain for some time. Now she was moving into the final phase of the cancerous disease that was destroying her. She was destined, however, to linger on painfully for several more months. Dr Trevaskis was now so distraught with his own grief at her condition that he felt unable to offer any solace to his grieving parishioners. So, it fell to his twenty-five year old curate, James, to minister to those in the parish affected by the *Titanic* disaster on his own. For many people in distress, for whatever reason, their parish priest was their initial source of help. Even if they did not approach him directly, notes would be pushed through his letterbox, children would be sent with messages to his door and neighbours would stop him in the street, to tell him of their concerns, for another family or individual in the parish.

Altogether the parish had thirty-eight families who had been affected by the tragedy. Only ten of these were to receive good news. The rest would all suffer the loss of a husband, father, son or brother. It was however, only five days since the ship had gone down and the current information available was not very reliable at this point. The parish contained official lodging houses, as well as men who boarded with families of workmates, and this helped to add to the general confusion.

It seems likely that the next morning, Saturday 20 April, the curate cycled down to the White Star Office in Canute Road, and there consulted the original crew lists, to find out which of his parishioners were likely to have been affected. By comparing these names, with the lists of survivors, posted on the railings outside the office, he should have been able to establish the families who would be in need of support. That he did this comparison between those who signed on and those who were rescued, seems to be confirmed by an almost exact copy of the 'Ide' signature, the curate reproduced in his diary list. This must have come from the original crew list, because both the original signature and his copy can both be read as 'Fell', due to the untidy letter formation, of the original.

No doubt it was this painstaking comparison, between those who signed on and those saved, that caused him to make his doleful list marked, 'Titanic Mourners'. These were the first homes he would visit. Other lists followed in the diary, 'Titanic Victims', and then just 'Titanic'. The lists continued over the weeks. Initially the sight of familiar names, like young Leonard Hoare who was a regular communicant at St Luke's, and fourteen year old Frederick Hopkins, an enthusiastic Scout with a sense of responsibility, must have unsettled him considerably, but as time passed shock gave way to dealing with the practicalities of life for the relatives.

James probably did not know all the men's names, so he concentrated on the addresses they had given when signing on; at least he could be sure which roads were in his parish. Logically these would be the addresses where bereaved family members could be found. Looking down the finished list of names, he saw some he knew but others were unfamiliar, either these men lived elsewhere and were boarding locally for a few days, or they were newcomers in the town looking for work on the liners. Familiar names were there; Hopkins, Hoare, Shepherd, Humphreys, Long, there were two Chittys at the same address...the list went on.

As well as contacting the families, there were the memorial services that needed to be planned. The main one for the town was due to take place at St Mary's church on Saturday 20 April. At St Luke's it was decided to have a memorial service for the children to attend. Space at St Mary's had apparently been limited, as shown by Winifred's single invitation, to only one family member and therefore no provision had been made for children to take part. At St Luke's church Sunday afternoons were usually devoted to a short children's service. On 21 April this would now become a memorial service, intended not only for those children directly affected by the disaster, but the unaffected children as well. This would help all the children to understand what had happened.

The families in St Luke's comprised about sixty percent of men from the victualling department and forty percent engineering crew. As already noted the stewards and cooks, together with their associated kitchen staff crewmembers, were not essential to the physical working of the ship and rarely held a seaman's rating. Therefore, they were not considered suitable crewmen to be in charge of a lifeboat and their chances of survival were minimal. Similarly if the stories circulating around the town about the engineers, firemen and stokers remaining below decks to keep the ship's generators running until the very last moments were to be believed, these men would have been among the last to come up on deck to take their chances in the water.

These were the men who worked in the worst conditions on board; intense heat, hard manual labour and clouds of coal dust in the air they breathed. They were among the better paid members of the crew, earning on average six pounds each trip. No doubt this rate reflected not only the degree of risk associated with their work, but also how essential they were to the ship. They kept the engines running and maintained the electricity supply to the vessel. The role of the coal trimmers was almost as important. Working in conditions akin to a coal mine, the trimmers maintained the 'trim' of the ship, moving the coal in the bunkers to maintain a supply to the boilers in the engine room and, at the same time, keeping the ship balanced (trimmed) so it did not list to one side or the other. These were some of the toughest men on board, they worked hard and they played hard; drinking, gambling and womanising; all activities which no doubt were taking place in the St Luke's area, if the number of public houses can be taken as an indication of such pastimes. The young curate had no illusions

FIGURE 10.2

The altar at St Luke's as it was at the time of the Titanic *tragedy. The tile mosaics surrounding it were later covered by curtains.*

(Courtesy Southampton City Archives).

FIGURE 10.3

It was not unusual for the church to be filled to capacity for Dr Trevaskis's sermons

(Courtesy Southampton City Archives).

about the nature of some of his flock; he recorded a fraudulent attempt to claim poor relief and another man as being a wife-beater despite suffering from consumption himself.[34] In such circumstances the wives would often find themselves short of money, even when their husbands were working but now, after the various strikes which had taken place over the last months, many were in dire financial straits. Nonetheless, it was one of these hardened men who had survived the disaster, a fireman named Dillon who, when criticism about the actions of the stewards during the sinking was printed in the press, spoke up in their defence remarking in a press interview, 'By God, those stewards were brave men and died game'.[35]

Complex family networks, caused by the death of marriage partners, or a parent, remarriage, illegitimacy and common-law partnerships often resulted in crewmen supporting, or partially supporting, a variety of individuals. In these situations the death of the crewman meant there would be little assistance for his widow from her immediate family members, since they too were in reduced circumstances. In comparison with these women Winifred was in a much better situation despite her father's weakness for the bottle. At least he and her brother, William, were now both working regularly and Martha, her mother, would ensure they contributed to Winifred's and baby Teddy's support. Moreover, they all had a stable home, whereas in the St Luke's area living arrangements could be flexible.

As had happened with Fred and Winifred, married sons and daughters frequently lived with one or other of their parents. Moreover, in an age when it was usual to rent furnished accommodation, it was easy to move home, as shown by John Diaper's situation. When he signed on the *Titanic* he gave his address as 102, Derby Road and sent two telegrams to the same address, to tell his wife he was safe. The second one was dated 28 April. However, when James visited on 24 April he was told that Mrs Diaper had moved to Northumberland Road, so apparently even John Diaper was unaware of an impending move, when he signed on. When, however, he collected his outstanding wages of one pound four shillings (120p) on 30 April, Diaper now gave his address as 181, Northumberland Road, having discovered his new address on his return.

All these factors contributed to the difficulty of the task facing James as he began the melancholy round of visits, to support his affected parishioners. As he visited the bereaved households, he was probably unaware of the problems he would encounter during the weeks ahead. The situation in every family was different and the results of their loss varied for each home. One thing was painfully clear, however; many of the men lost were not much older than himself, whilst others were teenagers who had only recently left school.

Over the coming weeks as he continued his parish visits, he gleaned more information, not only from the bereaved families but also from returning survivors, more accurate newspaper reports and other parishioners. Gradually the stories began to unfold; families stricken by hardship; men who had left other employment tempted by the glamour of the big ship; those who had left other towns and cities to sign on, hoping for a better future and, above all else, the stoicism of the women left behind to face an uncertain future. Most of them, like Winifred, would never know how their men died nor have the solace of knowing their bodies had been recovered and given marked graves. The young cleric wondered which was worse; knowing how the men had met their deaths, or the never-ending uncertainty. The Shepherd family in Bellevue Terrace, seemed to have the worst of both situations.

Thirty-year old Jonathan Shepherd had signed on as Assistant Second Engineer and returning survivors recounted to his widowed father and sister Ruth how Jonathan had died whilst on duty that night. After the collision he and three other engineers, Barrett, Harvey and Kemish, had rigged pumps in boiler room number five where unfortunately, Jonathan had slipped and broken his leg. His colleagues helped him to the pump room and left him there. Shortly afterwards the bulkhead in the pump room was breached, and when the others returned to help him, Jonathan ordered them up the gangway ladder. He was left helpless as the water rose rapidly around him; his body being trapped in the lowest levels of the ship, was never recovered. His three colleagues all survived. Jonathan's father and sister became dependants of the Titanic Fund, probably being helped to make their case by James; they received a total of sixteen shillings (80p) per week.

Helping his parishioners to register claims and writing letters on their behalf, not only to the Fund Committee but also other sources of potential relief like the local poor relief organisations, would take up a substantial part of James's time over the next few months. It was a subject, which the young clergyman found himself having to discuss repeatedly, with his bereaved parishioners. He would need to grasp the intricacies of the Fund's requirements in order to help the families with their applications.

One such claimant was Mrs Ide in Lyon Street. Burdened with her three young children – the youngest was just over one year old – and with another baby due very soon, her future was very uncertain unless she could get an adequate income for their needs. The new baby would never know its father and probably none of Harry Ide's other children would remember him either. It is likely that, with the needs of the young children, the house exuded the odour of damp and drying washing, mixed with the smell of cooked vegetables; evidence of the struggle to maintain cleanliness and provide meals, often within

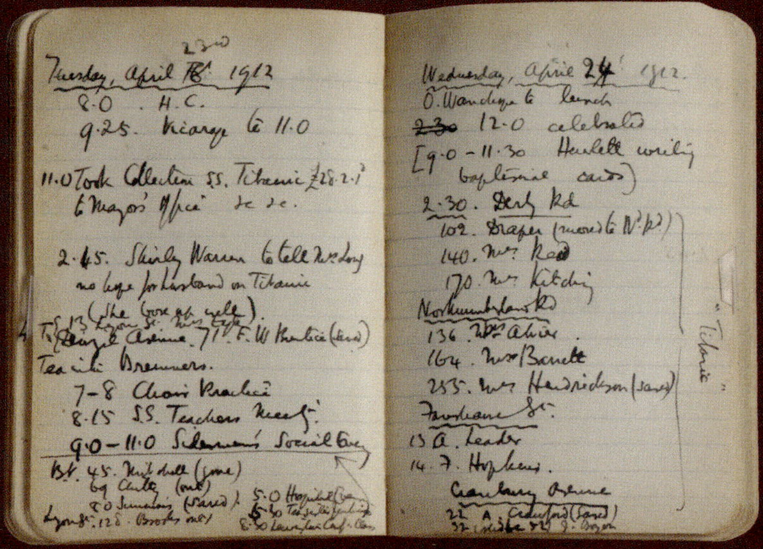

FIGURE 10.5

The Reverend Beaumont James's diary records his visits to his bereaved families and his visit to Mrs Long to break the news of her husband's death.

(James Family Archive).

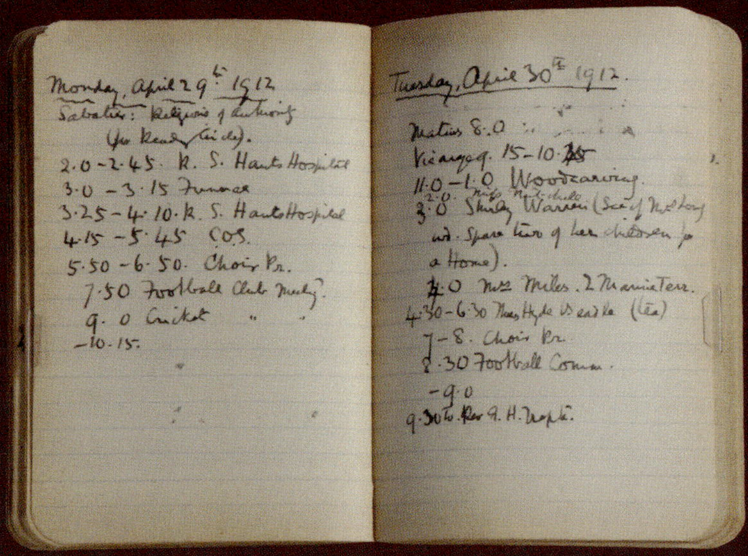

FIGURE 10.6

The suggestion is put to Mrs Long that she should give up two of her children.

(James Family Archive).

cramped living conditions. Such a potential mixture of aromas would have been familiar in the homes of most young families in the parish and James had become used to their living conditions. Ethel Ide, however, was a resilient woman and faced the future with determination. A fact that was confirmed, at the new baby's christening, on 28 July 1912. Beaumont James baptised her new child with the confident name for the future of Ernest Hope. Mrs Ide made an application to the Titanic Fund which gave her a weekly income of two pounds one shilling (205p). Perhaps she considered that her 'earnest hope' for the future had been realised with this allocation of money. It was a regular income; unlike her husband Harry's earnings as a ship's steward, which could suddenly stop if he had been unable to sign on for a ship or, as shown by Fred Simmons's letters, be reduced considerably if passengers were not generous with their tips.

Further down the street the situation for the Hoare family was different. They were regular churchgoers and young Leonard had been a familiar communicant at St Luke's church together with his parents. His younger sister Hilda and the youngest of the family, Sydney aged eight years, both attended the Sunday School. At seventeen years of age, Leonard had been independent since he left school and was an experienced steward from the *Majestic*, when he signed on with *Titanic* at Belfast.[36] Returning to Southampton on the ship, he signed on again for her maiden voyage. As with most single people still living at home, he made a contribution to the family finances, which meant that his mother, Sarah, was eligible for some payment from the Titanic Fund. Her husband however, was still alive and providing an income to support her and Leonard's two siblings, so she was given seven shillings and sixpence (37p) per week, an amount which may have equated to what she had received from Leonard, when he was at home. However, since she was not a widow and also under fifty years of age, she would only receive payment for three years.

Lyon Street housed another family affected by the tragedy - the Eagles. Twenty-six year old Alfred Eagle lived with his widowed mother, Ellen, and three younger siblings. Like him, two of these were unmarried wage earners and the three of them together provided the household finances. As she had only one child at school needing support, as well as herself, Ellen would only receive five shillings and sixpence (27p) each week, the Fund Trustees estimating that she had a source of income already. This did not mean that she could not re-apply later, when her children left home and her income dropped, the regulations allowed for that situation. Since she was aged sixty-one the three-year rule did not apply and she would receive support until she was seventy.

The Barratt and Hopkins families both lost young teenage sons. James chose to visit them both on the same day, as they were in very similar circumstances. Arthur Barratt was fifteen years old when he signed on as a Bell Boy, leaving his printing office job to go to sea, like his marine engineer father. With his father, sister and uncle all employed and living at the same address in Northumberland Road, Arthur's mother Margaret would only be eligible for a small allowance of approximately five shillings (25p) per week from the Fund. Moreover this would only be paid for three years, because she was under fifty years of age.

Letitia Hopkins, mother of young Fred, would find herself in a similar situation when she made her application to the Fund and she too, would only receive payment for three years. Her husband Alfred, had served in the British Army for several years and their youngest child had been born at Lucknow, in India. Now, at the age of forty, Alfred was an Army pensioner, working as caretaker at the White Star Line offices, in Canute Road. His eldest child, Fred, was a well-known member of the St Luke's Scouts. Perhaps it was his father's talk of the new White Star ship that fired Fred's imagination, but coming from a background with a sense of responsibility, when the possibility of adventure and opportunity for travel beckoned, then the attraction of the great liner proved too much and lying about his age, he signed on as a Plates Steward.

So the ship had claimed two of the youngest members of the community, teenage boys not long out of school and with all their potential unfulfilled. There was, however, one family which had lost two of its members, father and son.

At the turn of the century George and Julia Chitty together with their three children, Jessie, Archibald and Eliza, had lived in Earls Road, where George worked as a baker. Early in 1909 however, daughter Jessie married and the whole family appear to have moved to Bitterne. This may have been linked to the ailing health of Julia, because she died at this time. It is possible that this was also the period when George Chitty first went to sea as a ship's baker, signing on the *Oceanic*, where he would have known Fred Simmons. It was a logical career move. The liner trade in Southampton was expanding and becoming a significant factor – even the Yacht Laundry at Millbrook would change its name to Liners Laundry by the mid 1920s - the demand for crew seemed insatiable and gave the men who signed on some prospect of security. His new son-in-law George Carpenter, was a baker on the American Line mail ships and he seemed to be flourishing, which must have seemed to be a good omen for George Chitty's own future on the boats.

Archibald Chitty his son, had also decided to make his career on the liners choosing to become a steward, and he signed on with the *Adriatic*, the first White Star liner that had transferred from Liverpool to Southampton. Any previous employment security afforded by the liners disappeared, however, with the long-running disputes the previous year and the present coal miners' strike, which had been running since February. Father and son now moved from Bitterne and lodged together in Bevois Valley Road. It would be easier to reach the Docks from here. They would need to sign on early when the various recruitment stations opened for the *Titanic* crew. Twenty-eight year old Archibald signed on as a third class steward: his experience as a steward on her sister ship, *Olympic* would be useful. His father George Chitty, claiming to be forty-four years of age (he was actually fifty two years old) with his experience on the *Oceanic* as a baker, also had no difficulty signing on again, as assistant baker for the ship. Both father and son were lost in the disaster and therefore, when James called at their address, he did not find anyone there and it is doubtful that he knew the whereabouts of other family members. As George Chitty was a widower and Archibald was unmarried, there were no direct dependants and George's two daughters, Jessie and Eliza, were both married and presumably, had not been receiving any support from either their father or brother. Therefore, despite the devastating blow the two women suffered, there were no claims to the Titanic Fund, submitted by the Chitty family or their relatives.

Other families in Bevois Valley Road were also affected. Living in Marine terrace, about half way down the road was the Long family. Theirs was one of the most daunting cases in the parish. When William Long and Ethel Abbott were married, at the church of St James in the Docks in 1897, they both gave their ages as twenty. At that time he had been a fishmonger but, like the Lucrafts, he had been badly affected by the amount of unemployment in the town during the first decade of the twentieth century. Turning to the ships as a means of support for his family, but lacking any relevant trade or skill, he was obliged to become a coal trimmer. Now, at thirty-three he looked considerably older, reflecting the results of his years working in the ships' coal holds. During the coal strike he had been able to get very little work and this had made the family's situation desperate. With the imminent birth of their fifth child his success at signing on for the *Titanic* must have seemed a real lifesaver.

This was a family already under considerable stress; James had visited them several times already. On 25 March he had gone to visit Mrs Long twice. The first call had been at 8.30am in response to an urgent message received early that morning. Already sick and heavily pregnant, Ethel Long was now trying to cope with her sick, paralysed mother-in-law, as well as her own four children. He returned later in the day and saw both women again.

During his time in St Luke's parish the young curate had already forged links with the local hospital and individuals involved with poor relief in the town. A Miss Carey appears to have been one of those individuals. A middle-aged, unmarried lady she lived with her widowed father, Major General William Carey, in Archers Road. The curate had a long meeting with her, after recording a case of wife beating, which suggests he was seeking her advice on the matter. She became involved with the Long family later, so he may have approached her for help on their behalf on 25 March, before he returned to see the two Long women later the same afternoon. It is very likely that even if he did not see Miss Carey, he did consult with someone else who was involved with poor relief and could provide help for the family.

The curate continued to be concerned about the family and visited Mrs Ethel Long again on 1 April. On this occasion there is no mention of the paralysed Mrs Fanny Long, suggesting she may have been taken into care elsewhere, or returned home to Hill Street. She had been widowed the previous autumn, when her husband had died suddenly. Whether this shock had brought on a stroke, or whether she had a longer history of paralysis or partial paralysis, is unknown, but this was a family already in desperate need. Little support or help could be expected from Ethel Long's own immediate family, the Abbotts, as some of them seem to have been in St Mary's workhouse already. At some time during this period, possibly just after the *Titanic* sailed, Ethel was taken into the Shirley Warren Infirmary, which was itself linked to the workhouse. When James visited her home on 22 April he found Mrs Wisdom there. She appears to have been an aunt staying there to look after the children and usually lived in Ryde Terrace in Chapel, about thirty minutes walk away. No doubt it was the imminent birth of her fifth child, Jack, that caused Mrs Long to go into the Shirley Warren Infirmary and the baby was born shortly after her admission. However, being in the Infirmary when news of the disaster reached her, she was unable to check for herself whether her husband, William had survived or not.

Once again she turned to the young clergyman for help and he inspected the lists of those lost and those saved, on her behalf. On 23 April he returned to the Infirmary to break the news that all hope was gone and William Long, like many others, had been lost. The curate's diary records that 'she bore up well'. But Ethel Long's trials were not over yet. Finding someone willing to care for her four children while she was in the Infirmary was a problem. Neighbours could only offer a limited amount of help, no matter how willing they were; they had their own families to care for and there did not seem to be a quick solution to the Long family's problems. Six days later, James returned to see Mrs Long at the Infirmary, with the suggestion that she put two of her children in a Home. No record exists to say which ones were chosen, but in the Titanic Fund minutes for 29 January 1914 it is recorded that payments were still being made to Dr Barnardo's for two of Mrs Long's five children. It seems very likely that at the time of the sinking her children were being cared for by neighbours, because the curate went straight from seeing Ethel, to visit her next-door neighbour, in Bevois Valley Road, presumably to tell the neighbour, Mrs Miles, that arrangements would be made to accommodate two of the children elsewhere.

Whether it was as a result of his visits to Ethel Long, who may have voiced concerns about her mother-in-law, Fanny Long, but on 9 May 1912, the curate left his own parish to visit Fanny in Hill Street (later to become Hill Lane). Obviously she was not in a good situation because James, now immediately went to see Miss Carey, in nearby Archers Road, to ask for 'help for Mrs Long'.

Ultimately the Titanic Fund provided a measure of security for the family, supporting both Ethel and Fanny Long, together with the children, but initially their survival was probably substantially due to the efforts of Tom James's father, the determined young curate from St Luke's, getting support for the family from a variety of sources.

Despite the problems facing the families in the parish, it was still necessary to maintain the usual activities and commitments of parish life. The cricket matches for the choir cricket team still took place, and the Sunday School treat still had to be organised. At least one family of Titanic orphans joined the trip; Leonard Hoare's two younger siblings and possibly their mother, were given tickets for the excursion due to take place, on Thursday 20th June. The programme was organised and recorded in James's diary:

12.15 Assemble in School.

12.30 March to West Station

1.5 Special train to Lyndhurst Road

4.0 Children's Tea (*sic*)

4.30 Grown up's tea

5.15 Races

7.30 Reassemble; National Anthem; Slices of Cake.

8.10 Return by Special train

8.45 Dismiss at St Luke's Church

A comment at the bottom of the page says 'Showery to 4.30, afterwards wet day'. Regardless of the weather, no doubt the excursion was a welcome break for all those concerned and an indication that life went on. In the same way, life at Millbrook was continuing for Winifred Simmons, and baby Teddy.

St Luke's Church Newtown (Courtesy of Southampton City Archives)

CHAPTER 11

LIFE GOES ON

About two weeks after the sinking, there was a knock on the door of 263, Millbrook Road. When Martha Lucraft opened it, she found two men standing there, holding their caps and on the path behind them a large black box.

"Does Mrs Simmons live here, Missus?"

"Yes, she's my daughter, but she's unwell at the moment."

"We're Fred's mates from the *Oceanic*. He left his seaman's chest behind with us and we thought she ought to have it, now."

They shifted awkwardly and Martha asked them to bring the chest inside. It was large and bulky, the men had carried it from the Docks to Millbrook, a distance of approximately three miles. As they turned to leave, one said,

"We're sorry for what's happened, Missus. Tell Mrs Simmons we all send our condolences. Fred was a good sort".

Inside the chest were Fred's White Star waistcoat, his mattress and the piece of torn sheet music.

It may be significant that it was not White Star Line that arranged the return of the chest to Winifred, but Fred's colleagues. Shipping line owners were supposed to be liable for a 'heavy penalty' if they did not account for, or return, property belonging to a dead seaman. The fact that the return was not initiated through the official channels, again seems to reflect the Company's state of denial – if you ignored the problem, it would go away. A similar attitude seems to have prevailed over the belongings collected from the bodies. These had been collected and placed in bags labelled with the number assigned to the body, by the undertakers. In the case of identified victims, the items were returned to their families, but the many unidentified bodies' belongings were packed up and returned to White Star in the U.K., directed to either the London or the Southampton office.

Logically the belongings could have been used as a means of identifying victims, by asking relatives if they recognised any of the items. Whilst the Company may have argued that this could lead to theft by wrongful claims, the possibility of identification should have taken precedence. However, the course of least resistance and masterly inactivity prevailed; White Star apparently did nothing about the boxes of unidentified belongings. Their viewpoint

FIGURE 11.1

Teddy aged one year, looking fit and healthy, despite his earlier fall from the pram.

(Simmons Archive)

is easy to understand – the boxes possibly did not arrive for several weeks, or even months, so why bring the disaster to the public mind again, by advertising the need for their identification? Why cause more distress to the bereaved families? Why remind themselves? Why risk another outburst of criticism? The returned belongings probably remained in store for many years, until possibly finally being destroyed.

Fred's returned chest however, was quickly put to good use by the ever practical Martha. It was ideal for storing, blankets, linen and baby clothes. The waistcoat was washed, ironed and replaced in the bottom of the chest; the music was repaired and incorporated into Winifred's own collection; the mattress was taken apart, the ticking being reused to make pillows and the straw burnt.[37]

Winifred took little interest in her surroundings or events, barely seeming to understand what was taking place. Teddy recovered from his injuries and by his first birthday in November is thriving and looks, in his father's words 'a very forward young man'. It may be indicative of Winifred's state of mind, that in the photograph, Teddy's shoes are on the wrong feet!

Her parents' move into Winifred's home was an inevitable consequence of all that had happened. John Lucraft continued working as either a steward or waiter on the *Olympic* for some considerable time which meant the two women were mostly on their own, coping with Winifred's illness and the inevitable forms and letters which needed to be completed if Winifred was to receive any allowance from the Titanic Fund. To apply for and receive something from the Fund was often the only hope, and would probably be the only means of support, for many of the bereaved families.

Public sympathy for the families affected by the disaster manifested itself in numerous fundraising events and collections, both great and small. The village school at Cheriton raised £2, a collection in the Lyndhurst Village Chapel sent £2-1-2d (£2.6p).[38] Church collections such as that from St Luke's in Northam, were one of the most significant sources of support. Money from communities affected by the disaster was always particularly poignant. On Sunday 21 April 1912, the collection from St Luke's, where twenty-eight homes were touched by the disaster, yielded twenty-eight pounds two shillings and one penny (£28.11p) which James the curate, delivered to the Mayor's Office. The single penny in the total is probably the greatest reminder of just how impoverished many donors were themselves. With many of them literally 'on the breadline' themselves, it is impossible not to feel respect for the generosity of spirit which managed to find a few pennies, for those they perceived as having a greater need than themselves.

For others, especially the famous, it was possible to undertake fundraising in other ways: Sir Edward Elgar, Sir Henry Wood and Thomas Beecham all took part in a concert in London; composers wrote songs and the profits were given to the Fund; Thomas Hardy was among those inspired to write poetry; collections were made by Boy Scouts, trade unions, women's groups – all were involved with making donations to the Fund.

Eventually everything had been put in place, and by 19 March 1913 the total holdings stood at £413,212 – 2s – 10d (£413,212 .14p). This was after the European steerage passengers' families had been paid a one off lump sum; the bereaved Irish immigrant families had been paid approximately one hundred pounds each; all the administration costs associated with setting up the Fund had been met, and investments made to ensure a good rate of interest to produce capital every year. The first payments to the dependants were made on 15 January 1913 and it was estimated that the Fund would be entirely exhausted on the death of the last dependant.

The Fund's Southampton trustees also appointed a visitor for the bereaved families, to ensure they were coping and there was no hint of immoral behaviour or drunkenness, by the recipients. The administrators were not slow to suspend payments if they considered a recipient's behaviour to be unsuitable and anyone who went into the workhouse automatically had their payments stopped. Whilst this may seem unduly harsh, the administrators were only too aware that they were custodians for other people's money and felt it was their duty to oversee its use by the beneficiaries.

Moreover, they were subjected to regular scrutiny by the Public Trustee's Office themselves. This was a legal requirement for the administration of all charitable organisations. The Southampton Trustees Board, led by Philip Curry from the White Star Line, fought hard and long to prevent interference from the Public Trustee's Office in London. The Public Trustees would require payment for their services, from the Titanic Fund, and this would result in reduction of payments to the beneficiaries. Eventually the local Board had to capitulate, which was recorded with some regret. The Southampton Trustees were handling the largest portion of the Fund's money since most of the crew came from the town. This meant that their accounts were subjected to quarterly audits, whereas Liverpool and Belfast only had six monthly and annual audits respectively. This directly reflected the amounts of money each port was distributing and the number of recipients in each area.

Neither Belfast nor Liverpool appear to have required a full-time visitor to help care for the needs of the families, but Southampton did. Miss Newman was appointed as the Fund's visitor and she came once or twice a month to visit Winifred and Teddy, cycling around the

FIGURE 11.2

Winifred with four-year old Teddy. She is wearing a stylish suit and muff that she made herself.

(Simmons Archive)

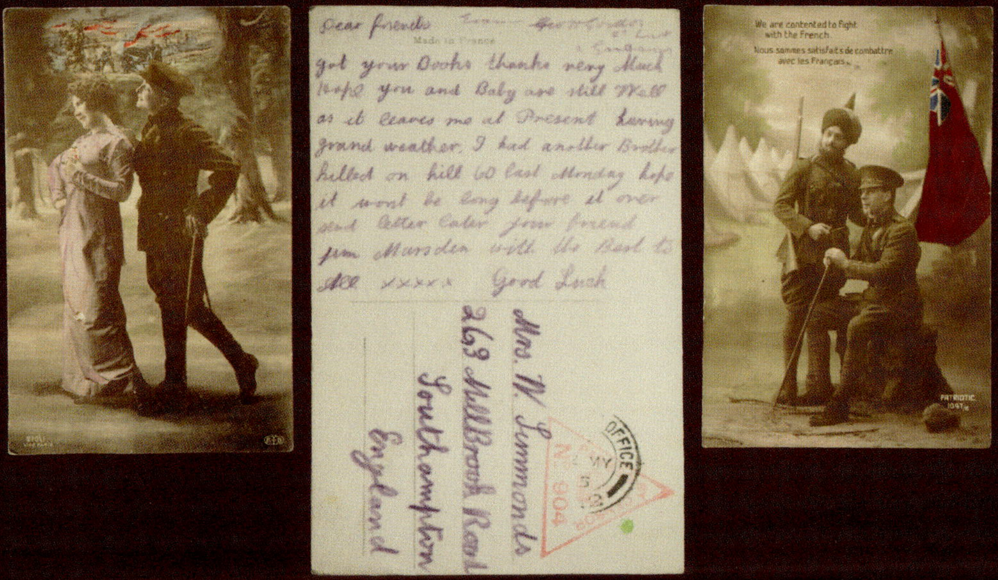

FIGURE 11.3

Three of the postcards Winifred received from Jim Marsden, from the front, during the First World War. The written message refers to the death of his brother on Hill 60.

(Simmons Archive)

FIGURE 11.4

One of the many pieces of music written in response to the tragedy.

(Authors' collection)

town on her upright bicycle, often with her Dalmatian dog running alongside. The little family Fred Simmons left behind were just two of the one hundred and eighty-two widows, three hundred and fifty-two children and two hundred and eighty other dependants supported by the Fund locally. Extra payments could be applied for, if a special need arose. Requests for dental treatment, including sets of false teeth were not unusual. One partial dependant, Mrs Bishop, applied for and received five pounds to buy a sewing machine. No doubt she used it not only to provide clothing for herself, her widowed daughter and grandchildren, but also to earn a few extra shillings for herself. Since she was the crewman's mother and therefore, only a partial dependant, she could not expect her allowance to continue for life, but only until her seventieth birthday. She was probably preparing against this eventuality by requesting the sewing machine.

Winifred appears to have applied once only, for an extra allowance of one pound, but no particular reason for the request is given and it was granted without comment. Most of the women's applications were for shoes, or other items of clothing either for themselves or their children.

Weekly payments were calculated on the needs of the crewman's family and the number of dependants or partial dependants he had supported. This was also apparently linked to the possible support the claimants might be able to expect from other working family members, and the wage that the crewman had been allocated, in his original signing on agreement. Other sources of unearned income, like disability pensions already available to families, were also taken into consideration and deducted from any estimated allocation from the Fund.

Exceptional factors were also taken into consideration; whether a child needed special schooling or care; if a child showed a talent then the Fund would pay for extra tuition, for example music lessons; children already in private schools would continue to be supported. In extreme cases of sickness as a result of the disaster, some survivors were also supported. Where individuals were either already, or later on, placed in various institutions like hospitals or charitable homes, it appears that the Fund trustees made payments direct to the institution. Thus some individuals do not always appear in the payment schedule, which gives the impression that they were not sustained by the Fund, whereas the reality was that they were being supported indirectly.

Although some of the regulations may appear rather draconian there was one provision which Southampton Local Committee seemed to apply regularly – they had discretionary powers to vary allowances according to the dependant's situation, in other words the rules were very flexible.

When all the relevant circumstances had been taken into consideration, the applications from crew memebers' families were allocated into one of seven categories (A – G); Winifred and Teddy were placed in Group D. Each category of claimants had its own scale of payments, covering the widows and how many children they had; whether there were one or two dependent parents; whether there was both a widow and dependent parent(s); were there any dependent siblings. There were even some arrangements made for 'common law wives', illegitimate children and, in a very few cases, payments were made to survivors. According to the *Daily Mail* 5 October 1912, dependants could expect a grant approximately equal to half the victim's income, which would have given Winifred about twelve shillings and sixpence (62p) a week. Instead she was allocated one pound three shillings (£1.15p), which was more or less equivalent to the amount Fred would have been paid officially on the *Titanic*. His wages would have amounted to one pound five shillings (£1.25p) per week, so Winifred's allocation was only marginally less than his full wage. The Fund Trustees therefore, had ensured that Winifred had a regular weekly income, which she collected using the Titanic Fund cheque book she had been given, drawing the money from the London and Provincial Bank near Holy Rood.

During this time help appeared in the shape of a young man, Robert Baker, a friend from Winifred's teenage years. Bob worked for the London and South Western Railway (LSWR), in the Docks, which were owned by LSWR. He became a regular visitor at Millbrook Road, taking Winifred and Teddy for walks and developing an affection for the toddler; as shown by the postcards sent to Teddy, which formed the basis for yet another postcard collection.

Although Winifred could be tempted out, it was nearly two years before she responded to her surroundings with real comprehension. Her mother, Martha, took her to see the Fleet Review in Southampton, in the build up to the First World War. When the reason for such a large gathering was explained to her, Winifred's reaction was simply, 'War? What war?' This seems to have been a turning point and from that time she slowly began to recover her spirits.

At this time, for unknown reasons, Winifred's father John Lucraft, went to New Zealand. He may have been tempted by the fact that the Shaw Savill and Albion Company were now using Southampton as the disembarkation port for their London – New Zealand – England route. Also, owing to the impending war, there were fewer opportunities for work on the trans-Atlantic ships, due to danger from the patrolling U-boats, and because many of the ships had been requisitioned as troop carriers. In 1914, having safely reached New Zealand, he remained there and set up his own hotel business. Communication with the other side of the world was difficult under normal circumstances, but now it was slower than ever. The two women were alone, only having their own resourcefulness to sustain themselves and Bob Baker's interest must have been a great help.

FIGURE 11.5

The Lych Gate of Holy Trinity church at Millbrook, shows its rural setting in 1917. The local 'bus passengers include a soldier in uniform on the roof, note the ladder for the roof passengers to ascend and descend.

(James Family Archive)

FIGURE 11.6

Inside Holy Trinity, where Winifred Simmons and Bob Baker were wed by the Reverend James Lyne Beaumont James. On the wall to the left, out of view, is the memorial to the men of the parish lost in the Titanic, *where Fred Simmons's name appears.*

(James Family Archive)

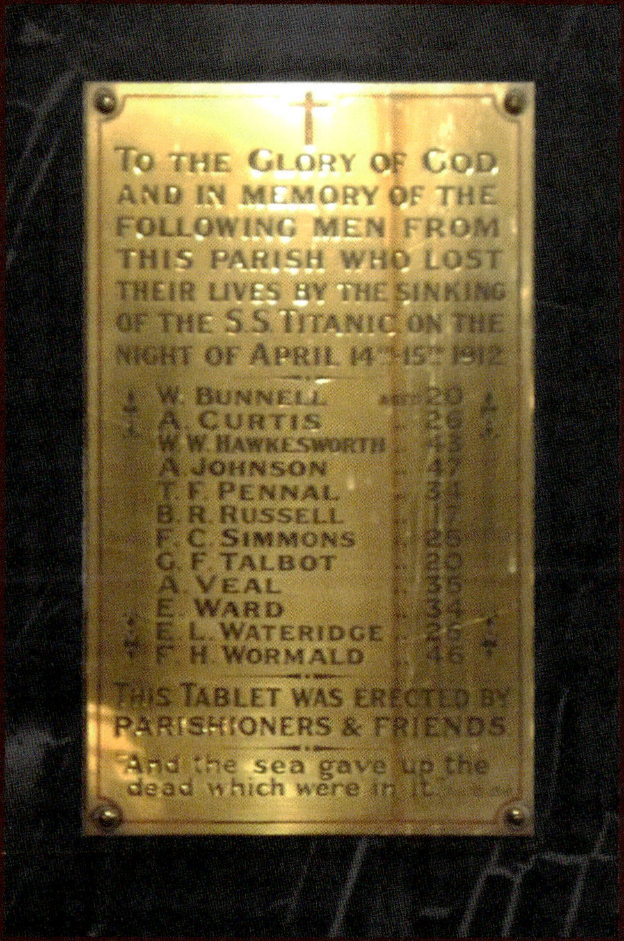

FIGURE 11.7

The Titanic memorial plaque inside Holy Trinity church.

Meanwhile the great wave of patriotism in support of the 'war effort' was making itself felt and Winifred, at last, began to respond more positively to events taking place around her. Women at home were encouraged to participate in work to support the men fighting in the trenches; they became drivers, nurses, factory and munitions workers producing the armaments to be used by the army and navy in the European conflict. Possibly for many of the young women bereaved by the *Titanic* disaster, this was an opportunity to gain some financial independence at last, others like Winifred supported the war effort in other ways.

One of the more personal methods of supporting the troops was to send them parcels of 'home comforts', hand knitted socks and gloves, magazines and newspapers from the U.K. together with letters.

So once again, Winifred took up her pen and began to write, but now she was writing to two young men stationed in France and Belgium. One was her old friend, Bob Baker, the other was a stranger, Jim Marsden, an infantryman in one of the northern regiments. She seems to have sent an open letter with her first bundle of magazines, to which Jim Marsden replied. It is hardly surprising that later letters written by Winifred, in the archive, reveal her as being a skilled writer with an engaging style and the ability to recount the details of everyday life with charm. No doubt this was a technique she had learned through her long years of writing to Fred sustaining their long distance relationship. It was a style to which both young men readily responded. Bob Baker replied with letters to Winifred and a variety of postcards to Teddy, from 'Uncle Bob', some of which were censored to prevent Bob's location in France becoming known.

Only four postcards from Jim Marsden survive, but they tell their own story of a young man full of optimism and determination, refusing to be disheartened by the conditions in which he finds himself, but slowly becoming inured to the horror around him. Almost as an aside he remarks, "I lost another brother on Hill 60 last week", such factual understatement underlines the hideousness of the First World War as much as any statistics. Frank Marsden is recorded as a casualty on Hill 60 in 1916. On the last postcard to Winifred, Jim's usually small, neat handwriting deteriorates, indicating it was probably written under difficult conditions, he ends it by saying, "I may not be able to write for a while". J. Marsden is recorded in the casualty lists a few weeks later.

Presumably Winifred would not have known of his death for many months – if she ever knew at all – she was not a family member, so she would not have been officially notified. There must have been a sense of *déja vu* to the situation, similar to the days of suspense after the *Titanic* sank. This may well have influenced her reply to Bob Baker when he proposed to her,

"Yes, if you come back from the war".

There may have been other more practical considerations for her reply, as well as not wishing to be widowed again. According to the rules of the Titanic Fund, if any of the widows remarried, they would no longer be eligible for an allowance from the Fund. On remarriage, they would receive a wedding payment equal to an amount up to, but not exceeding, a year's allowance and then all payments to them would cease. They would now have a husband who would support them and so the Fund's duty towards them was finished. Therefore, if Winifred had married Bob and he had been killed during the war, she would have lost her income from the Fund. However, all payments to the crewmen's children would be maintained after the widow's (their mother's) remarriage. It must remain a matter for speculation, how many young *Titanic* widows were tempted into marrying a patriotic young man, going off to fight for his country, only to find themselves widowed again and without any means of support, except a small war widow's pension.

Bob Baker however, did return safely to Southampton and on 28 November 1917 he and Winifred were married. Both were residents of Holy Trinity parish at Millbrook and naturally chose to be married in the church there. At the same time her father, John Lucraft had returned from New Zealand, after yet another disastrous business venture and he gave Winifred away, before signing the register as a witness to the marriage. It was the first marriage to be officiated over by the new Rector Designate, the Reverend James Lyne Beaumont James. After his four years in the St Luke's curacy, he had gone to St Peter's in Bournemouth. Now he had returned to Southampton and would be officially inducted as Rector of Holy Trinity church, the following week on 1 December 1917. In March 1920 he baptised Donald, the first of Bob and Winifred's four children.

Despite all this apparent optimism, the wedding had taken place at the outbreak of the notorious 'flu pandemic, which was spreading across large areas of Europe at that time. Amazingly the Baker/Lucraft/ Simmons household at 263, Millbrook Road was untouched by the infection, despite deaths in neighbouring families. Nonetheless, with the war drawing to a close and the safe return of the men, the future was looking brighter for the family.

CHAPTER 12

TEDDY

> A few weeks ago a group of Boy Scouts were loading a truck – I stood back and the one in charge called out, "Let the old man cross the road!" For a moment I wondered who he meant, then realised, "He means ME!"
>
> I had never thought of myself as 'old'; 'getting on a bit', but not old.
>
> I crossed the road and looked back – a long way, to the 1930s, 1920s and maybe a little earlier...

Teddy's memory did go back a long way – to his toddler days spent in the row of houses known as Alpha Terrace. Situated so that the front gardens faced directly onto Millbrook Road, the houses overlooked the railway sidings, on the far side of the road. Beyond the sidings was the beach of Millbrook Bay, known as Western Shore. Here were the public tidal baths and the boatyards of the local fishermen, but further along lay the treacherous mud of Millbrook Creek, ready to trap careless small boys.

Teddy's first clear memories were the early days of the First World War, when his mother, Winifred wrapped him in a blanket, carried him outside to watch the columns of soldiers marching along Millbrook Road in front of their house;

> to hand out packets of 'Woodbines' to fierce looking Indian soldiers with beards and wearing turbans. Some were on a sort of cart – perhaps a gun carriage, drawn by strange looking animals; MULES! We were to see plenty of these in the coming years. The mules were also carrying parts of small guns on their backs, gun barrels, wheels and boxes of ammunition.

Throughout the next three years there was a constant cavalcade of tramping feet, clattering hooves and rumbling wheels along Millbrook Road. Teddy watched them all, either from his bedroom window or the garden gate; regiments marching from their camps in the New Forest, the Scots regiments disappointingly wearing khaki kilts instead of tartan ones, but marching nonetheless to the skirl of the pipes; gun carriages pulled by teams of horses; tarpaulin covered carts and wagons – the Red Cross ones pulled by the stolid mules; every soldier full of excited anticipation.

FIGURE 12.1

The view from 263, Millbrook Road, across the railway to the water. Later on the isolation fever ship, Adelaide, *would be moored out there.*

(Simmons Archive)

FIGURE 12.2

Propaganda throughout the First World War was aimed at raising civilian morale and encouraging more recruits. Postcards such as this were commonplace.

(Simmons Archive)

On December 31 1917 Winifred and Teddy joined the thousands of local people who turned out to see the iconic British weapon – the tank. The press had been sending stories home about the invincibility of the tanks and their importance for the war effort. Some of the damaged tanks had been rescued from the battlefields and these became focal points for raising money. Known as tank banks, each was given a name. The tank, at Southampton, was the first such bank and had been returned from the battlefield at Cambrai, in France and was named Egbert. Nationalism in the local population was not even tempered slightly by the shell hole in Egbert's front casing. Once arrived in the town Egbert was housed in his own marquee on the Marlands. Here he remained until 5 January 1918, when he trundled down through the town to catch a train to Swansea. During the tank's stay in the town it sold £143,000 worth of War Bonds and War Savings Certificates towards the war effort.

As the war progressed so Winifred and Teddy saw the long, white-painted hospital trains; every carriage bearing a red cross and every window blanked out, as they trundled by, on their way to the West Country. No laughing faces or cheery waves from these. And lastly more marching, or perhaps shuffling feet, as the columns of grey clad prisoners of war were shepherded directly from the Docks, on their way to prison camps in the New Forest; no cheering from the onlookers now, only silence.

Life continued against the background of the ever-present war, and neighbours were an important part of everyday happenings. Those, in Alpha Terrace, were no exception. Among these was Mr Godden the undertaker, at Number 257, who frequently assembled a funeral cortège outside his house; a glass hearse drawn by black horses with black draperies (no black plumes as Mr Godden considered these to be in 'bad taste') was followed by an appropriate number of carriages for the mourners. The whole procession would be gathered and inspected before moving off to collect 'the departed'. Number 259 was home to Mr and Mrs James who had two sons, one being a playmate for Teddy. At 261 were Mr and Mrs Benns, a kindly couple who took an interest in the little 'Titanic orphan' next door. Teddy remembered that:

> Mr Benns was foreman sceneshifter at the Grand Theatre. He was a big man and rode a tall bicycle with two crossbars, with a slow stately way of pedalling. At weekends he would fix a sort of wickerwork trailer to it and Mrs Benns would sit in this, with her sunshade or umbrella and off they would go, rickshaw-like to Bramshaw in the New Forest.
>
> He took me to my first pantomime. Through the Stage Door and back of the stage, into the theatre, put down by the barrier between the pit and the stalls and told, "Don't move until I come for you". Robinson Crusoe was sheer magic!

Next-door neighbours, on the other side, were the Bannell family, with three young daughters who used to bring Teddy home from school. Tragedy struck their family, in 1918, when Mrs Bannell died during the ‘flu pandemic; the following year the heartbroken Mr Bannell emigrated to Canada with the three girls.

Midway through the war, in 1916, Teddy had become a ‘Mixed Infant’ at Freemantle Church of England School, where the tight white curls and watchful eye of Miss Whitbread, the Infants’ Headmistress, ruled supreme. Here he learned to read and write, using his own small blackboard and piece of chalk. The children walked to school, some from quite considerable distances, but Teddy lived only about a mile away. However, for many the walking distance proved too much, when there was a heavy fall of snow in March 1917. The school log reported that only half the children had arrived that morning and this occurrence necessitated a telephone call to the main Education Office – obviously the use of the telephone was not encouraged, apart from emergencies.

One such emergency was the ’flu pandemic which killed Mrs Bannell. The sickness was so rife, affecting not only pupils, but staff as well, that the school was closed during October 1918. It reopened briefly at the beginning of November and then had to close again for another two weeks.

It was during this brief reopening of the school, that news was received of the Armistice signing. The school responded with a suitable sense of the historic occasion. On 11 November at 11.45am precisely, the pupils were all assembled and after the news had been given out everyone sang the National Anthem; the Headmaster gave a short speech; raised three cheers and then the children were given a half day’s holiday – a relatively rare occurrence compared with the many bestowed on Teddy’s father, Fred, during his days at the Eastern Board School.

By 1919 Teddy was seven years old and had been at Freemantle Church of England School for three years as a ‘Mixed Infant’, now he ‘graduated’, by ‘going up’ into the Boys’ School, which would educate him until he was fourteen years of age.

Prior to the First World War fatherless children had often been stigmatised and bullied at school, but by this time many children had lost their fathers in the carnage of the battlefields and Teddy was just one of many fatherless boys – in his own words “there was no jeering and no sympathy”.

In comparison with his father’s schooldays, in the 1890s, Teddy’s school experience was luxurious. Each class had its own teacher, the boys had shared desks of the standard bench design, there were gaslights in every classroom and most had a coal stove for heating. Now however, he had to learn to write on paper with pen and ink – mistakes could not be so easily rubbed out and pen nibs had a nasty habit of getting their tips crossed!

FIGURE 12.3

'Egbert', the first of the Tank Banks, was placed on the Marlands, from 31 December 1917 to 5 January 1918, to sell war bonds and certificates for the war effort. It arrived with great celebrations; bands, flags and speeches. During its week in the town it raised £143,000.

FIGURE 12.4

Cartoons were always a useful way to cheer the population and paint the opposition in a bad light, but this one does not seem to do much for the reputation of either side.

FIGURE 12.5

When the First World War ended, postcards again played a role to raise public awareness about the many disabled servicemen returning home and their needs. This one raised money for St Dunstan's charity, to support those soldiers blinded during the fighting, usually as a result of a chemical gas attack.

(All images Simmons Archive)

FIGURE 12.6

The three little Bannell girls, Lily, Muriel and Dorothy, who brought Teddy home from Freemantle school each day.

FIGURE 12.7

Teddy in his penultimate year at Freemantle school. He is in the middle of the back row of desks – easily identified by his glasses. The classroom had changed little when I was there thirty years later – it still used the gaslights!

One of the school's prized possessions was Admiral Jellicoe's flag, which had been on his ship at the Battle of Jutland and now hung over Mr Marshall, the Headmaster's, desk. As Headmaster he had no separate office, only a desk in the corner of one classroom. No doubt his presence was a great help with discipline, as he was the arbiter of the cane or, more usually, the ruler across the palm of the hand. Boys developed their own techniques to lessen the effects of the blows; a hair across the palm of the hand was supposed to be infallible.

Whilst the school curriculum still focused on the 3Rs other subjects were also introduced into the timetable. History and geography in particular, fired Teddy's imagination and helped him to develop a sense of history within his own time. Whenever possible he acquired mementoes of events and places, which the family network supported, by an assortment of postcards sent from a variety of places, over the course of years.

The school appears to have been innovative in its approach to the boys' education and, unusually for the time, arranged large scale school outings for the pupils. These were marathons of organisation and stamina for staff and boys alike. To avoid the charge that the boys would be missing valuable learning time, the outings were scheduled for the weekends, usually a Saturday. There was a set pattern to the outings – one was a New Forest ramble, which covered a variety of routes and sites each year and the second trip was to London, again incorporating educational and recreational venues, to give the boys a wide range of experiences. So innovative were the trips that they were often given considerable newspaper coverage after the boys' return.

The route and sights explored in the New Forest are exemplified by the trip arranged for 19 September 1919. One hundred and seventy boys embarked on the 8.50am train from Millbrook Station, and disembarked at Lyndhurst Road Station. From here they walked to Highland Water, the Knightwood Oak, Rhinefield Drive, back to part of Highland Water, Gretnam Wood with Clay Hill, Irons Hill Walk and the Bombing Camp at Beaulieu Road before returning to Lyndhurst Road Station and back to Millbrook by 5.40pm – having walked a total of fifteen miles. The entry in the school log remarked, 'The boys are very keen and walked splendidly, none of them dropping out'. It seems more likely that they were terrified of being left behind!

Since there were no copying machines pupils had to copy their own programmes from the blackboard, for each trip. Teddy kept his programmes for the London excursion in 1922 and the 1924 outing to the Wembley Exhibition. These give an insight into the expected discipline and fortitude of all concerned, but in particular the dedication of the staff, their understanding of the boys' interests and their responsibility towards their charges.

London trips were organised like an army campaign, a strict timetable was set up, and all the expenses calculated exactly. The boys paid the overall cost of ten shillings (50p) by bringing in their pennies each week, until they had paid the full amount.[39] On top of this they were allowed to take one shilling (5p) for lunch and a maximum amount of one shilling and sixpence (7½p) for pocket money. On the Wembley trip Teddy must have gone without his lunch in order to afford the official Wembley programme, which was an expensive two shillings and sixpence (12½p).

The school staff organised train reservations for the trip; this entailed two reserved coaches at least, set aside for the boys for both journeys; that is to and from London. The 1922 London visit was a mixture of cultural and pleasure activities; hence it began with a walk from Waterloo Station to Westminster, Whitehall and the Cenotaph, to pay their respects to the war dead. The school was very conscious of the concept of Empire, but also the First World War was part of these boys' own personal histories, so acknowledgement of its cost was important.

This was followed by a visit to the British Museum – all before lunch! The afternoon was spent at the Zoo, where they also had their tea, before heading to the Alhambra Theatre for the first house, at 6.30pm.[40] After the performance they walked around to see the new advertisements, which were springing up around Piccadilly Circus and the theatres, these were the 'sky signs' – quite literally the 'city lights'. Eventually they travelled by the Underground back to Waterloo for their return train home – the school log remarks that the 'boys spent some time on the escalators'. They arrived back at Southampton Terminus at 12.30am, to be met by a tram to take them back to Shirley. This seems to have been a free service provided by the tram company, as a contribution to the community whenever there was a special event/group returning late at night. The log concludes 'the boys were all safely home by 2am'. Presumably the staff had escorted the boys home before making their way to their own homes – probably on foot.

However, there had been one small problem with that particular trip: the tickets for the Alhambra never arrived at the school, but the theatre confirmed they had been sent and the party was expected at the Alhambra, so there would be no problem when they arrived. The tickets did arrive several weeks later – after being returned from Freemantle in New Zealand. Mr Marshall, the Headmaster, promptly put this to good effect as an exercise in correctly addressing envelopes.

It seems hardly surprising that Teddy described Freemantle as a 'jolly good school', but his schooldays were rapidly drawing to a close and the Titanic Fund's last responsibilities

FIGURE 12.8

Teddy's last school trip – to the Wembley Exhibition, in London; shown are the expensive programme for the exhibition and a Wembley Lion souvenir, possibly a free gift for school parties.

(Simmons Archive)

FIGURE 12.9

After school was finished so Teddy's upholstery apprenticeship began, paid for by the Titanic Fund. The black, wooden toolbox by his side was the one provided by the Fund and stayed with him throughout his working life.

(Simmons Archive)

towards him needed to be addressed. Throughout his school years Winifred had drawn an income for his support, but now he would need a means to support himself and any possible future family he might have – a trade was needed, a good apprenticeship with a secure future ahead. Discussions took place between Winifred, the school and Miss Newman, the Titanic Fund visitor. Winifred was adamant that she wanted her son to have nothing to do with the sea, a good safe job on land was her main concern. Enquiries were made and Teddy joined Pasco and Pasco, an upholstery firm, taking up a five year apprenticeship to become a qualified upholsterer before serving a further two years as an 'improver'.

Part of the legal agreement for the apprenticeship stated that his parent or guardian should provide him with all necessary tools and clothing at the outset. These were paid for by the Fund, together with any fees for the apprenticeship agreement. The Fund had money set aside for each boy up to a maximum amount of thirty pounds, but costs were usually approximately twenty pounds. Teddy received a complete set of upholstery tools (many of which lasted throughout his working life), aprons and a new suit. He was now a wage earner, being paid a weekly amount of ten shillings (50p). The Fund's responsibility was ended and the thread to the *Titanic* broken. Or was it?

On his twenty-first birthday Winifred gave Teddy a bundle of old letters and papers, saying,

'These are all I have of your Father, they're yours now'.

EPILOGUE

THE THREADS CONVERGE

November 30th 1940

This was one of the worst nights of the Second World War for Southampton. Millbrook in particular was a target, due to the proximity of the shipping in the Docks. That night, as on the previous night, families huddled in their garden air raid shelters. Three families in the parish coped with the noise and shocks in their own different ways; the Reverend Beaumont James and his family in the Church Field Rectory shelter; the small Simmons family in their garden shelter close by the British American Tobacco factory, and Winifred Baker (as she now was) half a mile away, with her three youngsters in their shelter behind 307, Millbrook Road.[41] Her eldest son, Donald, was already in the RAF.

In the Rector's air raid shelter Dorothy James, his wife, did her best keep to the baby, born on 27 April, quiet and to occupy their other two young children. They had spent the previous evening in the shelter and had celebrated their eldest son's fifth birthday there; lighting the candles on his cake while the ground outside shook. Tonight the Rector kept himself busy by recording in his diary a minute-by-minute account of the raid. Both parents were thankful when, despite the almost incessant noise, the children fell asleep. During a lull, the Sister from Blighmont Nursing Home dashed across the road to check that the family was still alright and to reassure them that all was well with the patients in the nursing home. The ties with Blighmont were strong, having built up over a number of years and most of the James children were born there. The lull also gave the Rector an opportunity to view the devastation outside and observe the dull red glow over Southampton centre. The town had been subjected to a prolonged incendiary attack and the fire wardens and firemen were struggling to contain the flames. Electricity lines were down and water supplies were disrupted. When James recorded hearing a sound like stones on stones, what he probably heard was the broken electricity cables lashing around in the air, as they dangled from the broken pylons.

His account is disjointed in places, but this only underlines the stress of the situation:

> As I write a terrific air battle is going on above us – sirens 6.15 and immediately planes and gunfire – a heavy attack on So'ton at once developed – terrific explosions all around us – shrapnel like rain we thought they must have hit the Blighmont

> ammunition dump, a series of explosions for minutes close by – bombs are falling all around shaking our shelter to the foundations the effect worse than on Sunday week last and Saturday last – God be merciful to all...
> 7.37 seven severe explosions shook us – a plane dives nearly on us 7.39 – 2 explosions 7.46 lull – 7.51 planes again – 8.0 a lull - 8.8 zooms and guns – About 7.45 Sister Dan came over in the lull, stays till 8.7 - crackles, like stones on stones...

At 12.14 am he recorded three bombs landing in the water (Millbrook Bay) and that 'the white cockerel resented this and crowed...' The raid continued until 1.55am. To add to their problems it was bitterly cold and he records one and a half inches of ice, and no mains water, the following morning. He writes sadly in his diary for 1 December 1940; '...five brave women came to Mass – this the 23rd anniversary of my induction, how changed!'

How changed circumstances were for everyone, since he had performed the wedding ceremony for Winifred Simmons and Bob Baker, just days before his induction as Millbrook's new Rector in 1917.

Ted Simmons, who had been just six years old when his mother Winifred remarried, was now married himself, with a child of his own. Lily my mother, and myself aged sixteen months, were in the air raid shelter in the garden at Blighmont Avenue, together with our Staffordshire bull terrier, Patch. At this early stage of the war Ted was an air raid warden, so was on duty that night. Patch was under strict instructions from him, to 'look after Lily and the baby'. Both had been in the shelter well before the air raid warning went. The dog's acute hearing had heard the bombers well in advance and, as on earlier occasions, he had made a fuss until he had us both safely in the shelter. Patch's 'early warning' system also gave Lily, my mother, time to alert neighbours, so they too were in their shelters before the raid began. The night of 30 November 1940 was no exception; everyone in the little cul-de-sac was safely in their garden shelters. Ted reported for air raid warden duty promptly, while Lily sat in the shelter either knitting, reading, or writing letters to her family in Bristol and making tea on the primus stove. As usual, I slept soundly on the lower bunk with Patch curled up at my feet. A strangely tranquil scene set in the midst of the mayhem outside.

As the Rector's diary shows, the bombs were falling all around the area and Ted was kept busy in Waterhouse Lane where six houses were lost. It was not until quite late in the evening he heard news that a bomb had fallen in Millbrook Road near the *Sailor's Return* public house. Fearing the worst he hastened to his mother's home at 307, Millbrook Road. It was situated next door to the *Sailor's Return*. His fears were confirmed, their house had been damaged from the blast of two explosions along the railway opposite. The family comprising his mother, Winifred, and his three siblings, were all safe in their garden shelter but the house was mostly uninhabitable. Nonetheless, there was little the family could do; others were in far worse straits than they were. Therefore, for several months, they managed to sleep in the remains of the house and Winifred used their neighbour's kitchen to prepare meals, carrying them back to her children in the remains of their own home. Eventually the family was allocated accommodation in Testwood Road. Ironically it was almost directly behind 263, Millbrook Road where Winifred and Fred Simmons had set up home, on 6 April 1912.

Where bombs fell during the raids of 30th November and 1st December 1940 in the Millbrook/Shirley area. The boxed area shows where the three families were living during the raids.

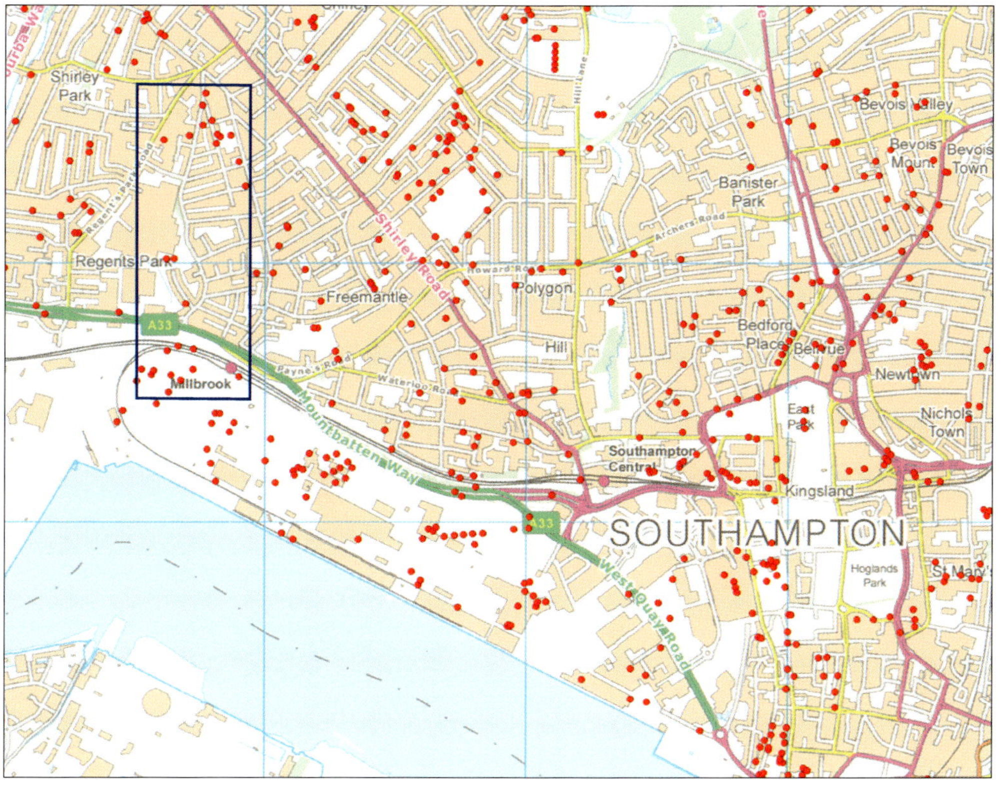

July 1983

Ted Simmons went to his writing desk and took out a bundle of old papers. He turned round and held them awkwardly. Lily glanced up from her knitting and looked at father and daughter,

'Your father has a favour to ask now you've finished all your research for your history diploma. He thought you might like something else to do.'

Holding out the papers to me, he asked,

'Will you find my father for me please, Mary?'

And so the search began with the bundle of letters from my grandfather, Fred, that Winifred and then my father, had cherished over the years. Slowly the story was pieced together.

February 2006

Mary: I see you contributed to *Titanic Voices*.

Tom: Did I? What's *Titanic Voices?*

Mary: A book produced from recollections about how the disaster affected the families of the crew and Southampton people in general. It was published in 1994.

Tom: Well, my father as a young clergyman had to break bad news to some of his parishioners who had lost family on the ship.

Mary: You *are* the right Tom James – that's the story in the book.

Tom: So what's your connection to *Titanic*, Mary?

Mary: My father, Ted Simmons, was one of the contributors to the book. He was raised on the Titanic Fund. His father, Fred Simmons, was one of the stewards and drowned in the wreck.

Over the years and generations the Titanic threads, in each family, had gone their separate ways unaware of the other's existence. Coincidence and spatial proximity gradually drew them closer together, until in one generation, they briefly touched and separated again. Now, in a later different generation, they met and new strands in Southampton's *Titanic* story were uncovered.

APPENDIX 1

Fred Simmons's Diary

Scene at a Revolution
Bueunos Aires
May 1st 5 04

It was a splendid day was the 1st of May in this certain part of the globe. As I was seated in the fore peak of our ship, with other members of our department arranging to go for a nice long walk, one of them proposed that we should play a football match. After a little consideration we decided to play. The teams were picked and at 2o/c we all went out to either play or watch a game of football A la Clyde.

The game started and a very pleasant one it was for a short time. All of a sudden strains of music reached our ears and of course we give the game a rest.

'Only for a minute', was what we said as we stopped, but it was one of those minutes which last from 2 hrs upwards or at least ours was and of course, the game stopped altogether. For what reason I will now endeavour to explain.

When we heard the music we thought at once that there was a festival of some description, so some of us went out of the grounds and made our way to Playa de Julia and there we stopped to see it pass. It was a grand affair until a certain society were passing a certain statue in the Playa.

Around this there were about 40 men and about 12 young girls none of them more than 20 years of age, they were all singing and shouting all sorts of evil things about the President. When called upon to be silent they shouted all the more and got more frantic than ever also shouting Morta les Presidente, which means down with the President. Again they were called upon to be silent this time by the Chief of the Police. During this stoppage the crowd got very thick around this statue and if you had sharp eyes you could have seen the hands going towards the pockets, also the knives etc going up their sleeves.

Well as I was saying the people were called upon to be silent, their answer was Morta les Vigilantes and as they sang this a shot was directed at the Chief of Police. However it did not strike him but it hit his horse, which cantered about in an agony of pain the shot having caught it in the flank. After this, all was a mass of confusion. Oh a terrible sight. There were men stabbing each other, children throwing stones at the Police, while me and two more were simply spellbound. Never did all my sins of my poor life pass through my head like they did then, for about a minute. I did not know what to do, for all around me and my two companions are a shrieking howling mass of people. Another shot rang out, this was from the Chief of the Police. It was fired in the air but as I afterwards learned, it was a signal, for in less than a minute there were from 60 to 80 mounted Police charging down upon the crowd, all of them with swords and pistolets in their hands.

I saw them hack their way through the howling mass, I also saw a few of them drop, not because I wanted to only I could not help it. It did not take us long to get out of the way, so off we went as fast as our legs could carry us over to the football field, we had t o go there to get our clothes, which we did in less than a minute. As I looked up the crowd were making for the docks and I with others, made for the gate so as to get out and down to our ship before the Police came our way, but luck was against us for as we reached the gate we found it was locked.

There was only one thing to be done and that was to climb over the fence which was the work of about a minute at the time. I also with a good few more, found that it was not the same wire at the top as at the bottom. The wire at the bottom was kind to us and let us go on our way but the wire up top wanted us to pay our footing. However, I could not stop to explain my reason for going that way. As I heard a distinct ping, on the wire below, after that over I went falling or flying I cant say which, once on a piece of sound footing it didn't take me long to find my way to the ship.

Just as I was going by the corner of the football field a terrible sight I saw, the victim of a most horrible murder was a poor foot policeman. There were about five men after him. One of them picked up a stone and threw at him, hitting him under the right jaw. As it struck him another one fired two shots at him. One hit him in the chest the other in the head just above the left eye. This was not all he had. The same one that fired at him ran up and took the poor policeman's sabre and stabbed him in the chest and stomach, also cut him across the face severing his ear from it. He then did more but it is to horrible to explain.

Well that was sight No 1. After recovering myself, I made on with the crowd to the ship but just as we got to the railway I for one, heard a groan and looking saw a poor little boy about 9 year old, lying against the woodwork of the bridge with a shot right through the head. Oh dear that nearly sickened me. I went on not knowing where. Getting borne on with the howling mass, now and again I would catch a glimpse of my two shipmates, also seeing men falling down, either shot or stabbed or fainting, it was a horrid sight. After having all the wind and nearly all the life squeezed out of me I reached the ship but I didn't stop to look for the gangway, I was over the side a bit smart.

I was no sooner there than dozens of others came over simply taking charge of the ship, I should say that there were from 800 to 1000 people aboard, they were in the pantry, saloon, cabins, galley and every where else. They were shouting, crying and squabbling about something awful.

Then all of a sudden another shot rang out and it hardly died away before a horse came galloping along with its master a policeman, fallen across its neck. The poor fellow had half his face shot away. That was all I waited to see and as I got to the Fore Peak there was a sound of panting men's breath. I look around and saw a few of our Stewards lying in their bunks as white as the sheets they were laying on and I am sure I must have been the same. I lay down on my bunk and for the first time since I started sea life, prayed and thanked the Lord in real earnest.

I did not see any more of the Revolution but as it was I saw more than I wanted to. What others saw would fill a book with a 1000 pages. A few went ashore after to have a look at the town and said it was in an awful state, windows broken, doors busted, pavements torn etc. I can remember no more so I will close hoping my account will interest you I remain

Yours Truly

F.C. Simmons
Stewards Dept
RMS Clyde
Darsina No 4
Buenos Aries
South America

Voyage on the R.M.S. Clyde

I will now endeavour to give you an account of misfortune which happened to the above named ship.

We left Southampton on the 12 March 1904, it was a dull day and as we got down the Southampton water we found it was going to be a bit rough.[42] After we left the Needles we made for Cherbourg which is in fair weather a 6½ hrs run and leaving Southampton as we did at 12 o/c we should have arrived there just before 7pm but it was so rough going across Channel that we did not arrive there until 2am on Saturday morning.

The little dusting down made us all wish we had not come away. We left Cherbourg at 5am Sat[urday] for Vigo where we should have arrived at 8pm Sunday. Having got outside Cherbourg breakwater, we encounter a strong S.W. wind with rough seas and as we got towards Ushant we got the full force of a S.W. gale.

The old ship was just like a cork. We were being tossed about dreadful. The seas came all over her, the wind howled and moaned. The ladies and poor children cried and everything was one mass of confusion. The water was knee deep on her main deck, the cabins were flooded and that scared the women more than ever. The cries of the children were heartrending. 'Steward, Steward', was what you could hear all over the ship. You would go to where the cries came from and ask what you could do and they would ask you if the seas are going down, and also ask you to stop and talk to them. Some poor wretches were dead sick. The look of agony on their faces told you what they wanted and that you couldn't get. 'I would give anything to get on shore.' 'Why ever did I want to leave my dear home?' 'What shall I do?' 'Oh I feel as if I shall die'. That was a few of the cries you could hear.

The weather did not get any better and we were beginning to think the Clyde had made her last voyage. We sighted Ushant at 12 am on Sunday and for 16hrs we could not pass it. The seas and weather were terrible. At times she would roll over and stay for 10 minutes before she righted herself. Those were the times when everybody's heart was in their mouth, because a ship that rolls at 45 degrees is not worth much because its a case then as to whether she goes right over or not and our old ship was rolling at 43-44 degrees and she scared the life out of everyone. Some of the crew were writing notes as best they could and putting them in bottles so that if the worst came to the worst, at some time or other they would be picked up.

For 3 days we had this weather and then it abated a bit as we got into the lee of the land and we arrived at Vigo 4pm Wed[nesday] to the delight of the passengers who were almost frantic with joy and very soon found their way on shore for a while, and a much needed change.

There were a few accidents our Captain was worse off. He was thrown by a sea right across the bridge and when picked up it was found that he had injured his arm shoulder and back. One of the firemen was badly crushed down the stoke hole. The 4th officer slipped and broke his wrist and had to be sent home also did the fireman. Several others were bruised and cut. the Ex Fra (?) waiter smashed his fingers. After a stay in Vigo we leave for Lisbon. We again encounter heavy weather and arrived there 8 h[ou]rs late.

We leave Lisbon with a large number of 3rd Class passengers. The weather was exceedingly rough the first 2 days from Lisbon and it was a horrible sight to see these Portuguese while they were sick. One poor fellow broke a blood vessel and died and was buried the same day.

The weather was a lot better after we left St Vincent C.V. and the other part of the voyage out was pleasant.

Homeward bound we have a very good start, we are on the mud at Buenos Aires and are delayed a day

We arrive at Monte Video and among the cargo is the corpse of a man which we have to bring to England. His wife was a first class passenger and she was at times nearly mad with grief and several times they had to lock her in her cabin.

We leave and arrive at(sic) we meet the Nile and we get letters and papers and read the news and all about the storm, which we were lucky enough to pass out of quite safe. We get to Rio de Janeiro and among our passengers for Purnambucco is the Vice Presid[ent] of the Brazils and a nice fellow he is.

We have a[n] anxious time a[t] Bahia. We have orders to bring an Italian prisoner home. We were told he belonged (the) a British steamer and that he had shot the donkeyman and wounded 5 others, among them the Captain. When brought on board our ship he was in a straight jacket and a nasty looking fellow he was more like a Brigand than a fireman.

Nothing of great interest at Purnambucco only the bands that came round to meet the Vice president.

Today our Chief engineer Mr Banks feeling a bit queer went to lay down and never got up again. The poor old fellow died after 7 day illness at 11.30am Tuesday. There was a 3rd Class passenger, a Spaniard which was ill all the time on board. He died a(t) 6pm the same day and he was buried at sea at 9pm the same night. They took the corpse of the Ch[ief] Eng[eer] to Lisbon and he was buried on shore the same day. We leave Lisbon in fine weather and arrive at Vigo next morning after leaving Vigo we have a fine run home where we were all thankful to get.

Hoping this will interest you
I remain

Yours Truly

F.C. Simmons
R.M.S.Clyde

Sunday Sport at Savanieia[43]

R.M.S. Atrato 15.5.05[44]

"Now then there! Come on, me lads!"
"Rise and shine, you stewards of the Royal Mail Line".
"Shake a leg.!"
"Come on now, you tired Hunks!"
"Up now and lets 'av ya!"

This was what was greeting us on Sunday at 4.45am.

Out of our bug-walks we got and our orders were to bath brick the Saloon out. After that finish for the day.

At 7.30 we had finished the Saloon and a few of us went to do a bit of fishing. After playing at this game for about an hour, we managed to catch enough fish for the cats breakfast and so we went on board for ours which we did not enjoy because it was leather and worms, which in other words means, a R.M. steak and Macaroni.

We all got over or under it and those who weren't ill came for a little more fishing. After a time fishing got too dry, so one of the Hunks, or Stewards, proposed bathing. Six of us agreed and away we went bathin. We were in the water for 2½ hrs and we did have some fine fun.

We got logs of wood and floated about on them and then for a change we played dab-touch wood. Which game made us swallow more water than we wanted to. After that we played a game of pyramids. Of course, you may not understand the meaning but I try to explain to you we were five together and well know as dare-devil Dicks from Sum-Sum. So now four put their arms at full length on each others' shoulders which makes the appearance of a ring and then the other one climbs on top of the arms and steadying himself dives or falls off.

This was a great success until one had a dive to many, that one was Simmo. He dived too deep in shallow water and he saw stars and all sorts of other thing for minute or two. When he did happen to feel feel his napper he had a slightly raised a bump. So much for the bathing.[45]

Now we go on board to our dinner which was passable. After that, those who had stopped on board in the morning told us they were going up the bush in search of orchids.

"Will you come?" one said. "Sure thing, Mike," was the answer of the renown five and off we go to the bush. An old fellow met us as we came off the pier and he was our guide. He took us to his hut and the five devils helped therselfes to knives and choppers and then we start and get to the bush about 2.15.

We had to plough our way through and we quite enjoyed it. One would be falling over the stump of a tree and another would be swearing because a branch of a tree had hit him in the chops.[46]

"Orchids! Orchids!",

"Where?" "Up in that tree". That was what we hear next.

So then the five started to cut the tree down. Hot work we found it, but at last the tree fell and we cut the orchids off and went on our way.

We saw several wild donkeys and of course we chased them. We also saw heaps of small snakes and lizards and one tigercat.

"Simmo! Where are you? There! Another orchid up in that tree!"

Taking my knife I went up the tree and started to cut the orchid down, when a slight rustling in the bushes below makes me start and down I came with a run and didn't stop till I reached the bottom. I was a bit scratched and found that the thing which made me jump was a young bird. After a time I reached the others and I was not sorry, for you could soon lose yourself there.

We got a few more orchids and then we made our way home. Reaching the guide's hut we sat down and had a drink and looked at the Atrato and thought of all the good people at home going to church.

When one of the five said, "Let's pinch that canoe,"

"And go for a row", agreed Pete and away we went and put the canoe in the water. After pushing off one jumped in, then two and a third and Simmo was in the bows. When a fourth came rushing at the boat he caught hold of the side and of course over we went with all our clothes on. Once wet, we intended to have some more fun. So one of the renown five took duck and we had fun to our hearts content and it pleased all on shore.

Wet through we had to go on board. We did not mind as long as none of the officers saw us. But our luck was out, for as we went up the gangway the first one we met was the boss.

"Had a good day, by the look of you", he said, "No more leave for you, my holy terrors".

After changing our clothes we all went and had tea and finally after a grand day's sport we retired to rest.

The renown five are the following
Star of the Atrato F.C. Simmons,
The Blue nosed Donkey A. Molloy,
Laughing Allpdes(?) H.Besley,
British Consul for the R.M.S. Atrato, the Hon Alf Waterman,
Chief of Liars His grace William Fry.
Hoping this will interest you

I am yours truly

F.C.Simmons
R.M.S.Atrato

Tour round the south East of England

August 11th 94[47]

'Got all you want, Ginger?'
'Yes. Have everything, Fred'.
'Right you are. Now away to go'.

We start and go over the Floating Bridge and so make for Bursledon Bridge, pay our toll and then stop and have a drink and then off again on the road to Titchfield. No accidents, but on the way to Fareham a dog doesn't like the look of Goggles and he haves a go at my leg. Off I come, a cropper and tear the knee of my trousers. Getting over that, we make for Old Shoreham where we arrive at 7.30pm. We now have to look out for a bed for the night.

The only thing we could get was a bed 6f[ee]t 4[inches long]. Very small for the two of us. We tossed up to see who would sleep under the sheets and I lost, so Ginger slept under the sheets and I on top. We did not sleep very well. We arise next morning at 6am, have our breakfast, borrow a needle and cotton and at 7 we are well on the road to Brighton.

We stop, have a smoke and drink and make our way to Eastbourne. We lunch here and off we go and get to Hastings at 4.30pm. We have another soda and milk, also a bathe and make tracks for Winchelsea but before we get there I have a puncture. We walked into Winchelsea and have it repaired also have tea. We then make a rush for Rye, but just outside Winchelsea I have another go. It was down a steep hill. I came off and into a hedge I went. On looking at myself I found I had a piece off my thigh also a very bad cut across the hand. An old man with a barrow remarked, 'Serves thee right'. Some women ask me if I was hurt and of course I said No, but still I meant Yes. However I managed to ride to Rye.

We could not find any accommodation there so we made for New Romney which was 14miles. It was getting dark and we had no lamps so we rode as hard as we could but did not get to New Romney that night.

After walking for ½ an hour we came upon a cottage and here we enquired if there was any cycling accommodation about there. A kind old farmer said there was not, so we had made up our mind to sleep in the hedge. We were just settled down when we heard someone calling to us, so we went back and found it was the old farmer. He said if we didn't mind we could have a bed between us at his cottage. We gladly accepted his offer and we were soon inside his home. Here we found a nice old lady who was very anxious to do anything for us. So we had a drink of milk to start with and then a wash and brush up.

After that I borrowed some rag and Ginger fixed my thigh up it was not at all painful, so we went with the farmer to a pub and had a drink after that we went back to the cottage and were showed our room. We soon found the bed and were not long in going to sleep.

Next morning we woke at 7o/c, washed had breakfast and left for Margate.

At Folkestone we had a bathe and it made me sit up for my thigh didn't seem to like salt water.[48] We arrive at Dover at 12.30pm have lunch and we got to Margate at 3pm. There not being anything to stay for we left for Canterbury.

On the road my pal haves an accident. I brought him some brandy and then he got some more and of course, he was very soon up the pole. After a good deal of trouble we got to Canterbury at 6pm. We found a hotel and stopped for the night. At 8am we leave for London.

It was a very hard ride, nothing else but uphill and down and after we left Sittingbourne it rained in torrents. We arrived at Gravesend at 4pm and after tea we left for London when we arrived at 6pm.

I found my friends at Camberwell and also left Ginger, as his home was in London. After staying the night in London, I left next morning for Southampton where I arrived at 3pm in the afternoon. I was 4½ days riding and covered 342 miles. Through neglect of attention to my leg I was laid up for 11 days.

I remain yours

F.C. Simmons

On the back page is a note :

Dear Sir
Please give bearer the parcel which I was going to call for and please could you write the prescription in English and oblige me.

F.C. Simmons
R.M.S.Clyde
DLL
B.B.

APPENDIX 2

BISHOP EDWARD TALBOT OF WINCHESTER'S ADDRESS AT THE TITANIC MEMORIAL SERVICE

St Mary's 20 April 1912

In spite of the spring sunshine streaming over us there is a pall of sorrow over the land and it lies thickest over this town and men's hearts turn to you in sympathy.

None of us perhaps, can remember a catastrophe so awful - such a plunge of change from ease and security to darkness and destruction, the coming suddenly, and by accident of such an agony of suspense, such torture of waiting in the ship for imminent death; or watching upon the bleak face of the water to see the end, such heartrending separation, such physical suffering of those who survived.

It is a thing to darken the imagination, to turn the brain and crush the nerves. You have scanned every detail of it. You have tried to picture what is altogether beyond any picturing of ours. You can not do less in honour and sympathy with the dead and living, but you must not linger there. You must not feed yourselves with horrors, but look up and come away.

Where can you run but to each other and to God? In a great common trouble there is wonderful and real comfort in great common sympathy and the sense that you are caring and grieving for one another brings some relief. But it is to the House of God that you bring your own and your brother's grief. It would seem almost better that you should be still and keep silence before Him. Certainly cheap words, easy phrases and fine sentiments have no place there.

Yet there are things that might be said which should be said. God speaks through such a tragedy unspoken words and you must try to spell out His meaning and speak of it to one another. He feels a great wish to be there amongst His people and to try to speak to them a word of comfort. Surely we have not been given only a 'fair weather' religion?

First a word as to the catastrophe. It is that which rightly appals us by its magnitude and scale. But I believe God meant it should be so. Yet each one of those lost lives had to die at some time and each Southampton home over which is now the shadow of death, must sooner or later be pierced by bereavement. Their case and your grief is the same, except that for the former death is past and ours is yet to come.

The coming together at one time and at one stroke of so much trouble is awful. But is it only awful? Can you think so when you see how you stand by one another and help one another?

Those of whom you think were almost cheated of the terror of the solitude of death, for they were not alone. Human fellowship, which is always revealed and deepened by great experiences was in power to the end. The hand which by noble instinct played 'Nearer my God to Thee', only gave voice to the common heart of all. Then what nobleness was wrought in them. What an opportunity they had and took. They have written new names upon the holy roll of the brave and the self-sacrificing. They have sent back to us across the Atlantic by spiritual telegraphy to stir, confirm and deepen what little poor courage, firmness and care for others, might be in our hearts.

It was an appalling death for them. It was, to not a few, an heroic death. Theirs was no empty word of faith of the bubble reputation; it means that in their last hours the God of their lives had His hand upon their lives. What men God wrought in those short hours to bring their nobleness to the required perfection to make them worthy of Himself. And in others of whom we might have the bitter thought, 'He was not ready to go'. Do we know what quick purification their souls passed through; and to what quick repentance they were brought as they waited minute by minute for the final plunge - a repentance not of cowardly fear, but of sharp and genuine sorrow. Perhaps their soul' s confession was heard, and the word of absolution spoken by God Himself in their hearts.

Nor was it only for them that God could work through such an awful doom. They suffered perchance for us.

For us there might be need of such a catastrophe. When had such a mighty lesson against our security , confidence, trust in the strength of machinery and money, been sent through the nation as now? How much more eloquently than by words, God has read to us that lesson. We cannot pass this by.

How can the waste, the cruel and wanton waste of money - which is needed on every hand for the bettering of life and the help of the needy - on the real wickedness of what our leading newspapers call the luxuries and hyper-luxuries, or in the senseless hurry of competition; how could that be a rebuke, as it has now been a rebuke? We cannot judge and far be it from us to judge this man or that.

But God by such an act compels us to think and see things in their true light. God grant that we and our sister nation America, might take the lesson to heart and profit by it!

The lesson was needed. Assuredly we needed it and needed it badly. The *Titanic* in name will stand for a monument of warning to human presumption. But let God rebuke, not we. Let no words of bitterness, complaint or recrimination tarnish the holy sorrow of the day. Do not be too much hurt and cast down by the catastrophe, for God has His ways in the catastrophes of the world as in the smooth and quiet times.

There are the grief stricken hearts of parents, widows and sisters who have lost those to whom they have given their hearts. It is not enough only to ask them to be patient. To them I would say remember the great example of Jesus Christ and the sorrows He Himself suffered, which in the end resulted in Him overcoming death and turning sorrow into gladness. The cross of Jesus is a sign of victory.

It is God' s will that your lost ones should have no earthly grave, no cross of granite or marble can be set where their bodies lie. But you can do for them a nobler thing. By the power of imagination and faith, you can set up on that bare bleak space of the Atlantic waters a great cross of commemoration, which would speak to us of their heroism and victory.

Let it not be in vain that they have died; but let us all follow in the paths of righteousness and become true sons of God; and by and by we will enter into eternal life and meet again those we have loved and lost awhile.

Endnotes

1. A. Patterson, *A History of Southampton, Vol III Setbacks and Recoveries 1868-1914*, Southampton Record Series, Southampton (1975). pp.122-4.
2. R. Douch, Visitors' Descriptions Southampton 1540-1956 *Southampton Papers No.2* Southampton (1978), p.23.
3. M. Doughty, *Dilapidated Housing and Housing Policy in Southampton 1890 – 1914* Southampton Records Series Vol 29 Southampton. (1986) passim.
4. This may have been the boarding house where friends of Jane Austen had lodged in 1808. (D. Le Faye, *Jane Austen's Letters* Oxford, (1997) p.160).
5. A. Patterson, *A History of Southampton, Vol II The Beginnings of Modern Southampton*, Southampton Record Series, Southampton (1971) pp.89-90.
6. A. Patterson (1975) p.107.
7. *Idem.*
8. VIP was an abbreviation used for the slightly ironical term, Very Important Person.
9. This was a keyboard instrument with large foot pedals that acted as bellows, when pumped by the player. The air generated then blew over metal reeds to produce the notes.
10. A. Patterson (1975) p 118
11. A. Patterson (1971) p.97.
12. Bathbricks were usually solid pieces of pumice stone used for scrubbing floors with water, to scour off the marks.
13. The term 'tip' apparently originated from the practice of restaurants leaving a plate out for donations from their customers, marked To Insure Promptness. This eventually became abbreviated to T.I.P.
14. This would have been equivalent to £2. At that time there were five dollars to one pound.
15. This is the date given in his account, but it seems to be more likely that it is the date he is writing the account. Evidence from his discharge book and newspaper reports of the storm indicate that 12 February 1904 is the correct date.
16. 'Dusting down' is an understated expression for a bad situation or incident.
17. The donkey was the ship's crane and the donkey man its operator.
18. Chief Engineer's name verified as Mr Banks who died on voyage on 29.03.04. Fred gives the day of the week that he died as a Tuesday; the 29 March 1904 was a Tuesday.

    All the other five engineers went up one rating and a boilermaker became the 6th engineer.

    Arrived at Vigo 31.03.04 - six Spanish waiters left here.

    Trimmer W Hartup rated up to fireman 23.02.04. Fred reports an injured fireman had to be taken off ship.

    Two AB Seamen marked with a red cross in list - seem to have finished voyage. Injured?

    Asst Bos'n, Carpenter and the Master of the Hold were all made responsible for Mrs Gear - distraught lady with dead husband?

    Newspaper reports of terrible gales in Channel, ships turning back and seeking haven in various ports. The Union Castle liner Pembroke Castle had run into severe weather getting to Ushant - the journey lasted three days and nights - and then it had worsened. The Dover telegraph station was damaged and unable to operate. The storm seems to have lasted about a week and extended out into the Atlantic. *Southern Daily Echo* various reports throughout the period 4 February 1904 to 10 February 1904; *Hampshire Chronicle* 5, 12 ,19 February 1904.
19. Southampton West station was not rebuilt as Central Station until 1936.
20. Although the crew list states a monthly rate of pay, in reality this was his pay for the three week trip.
21. This seems to have been the direct opposite from the usually accepted acronym POSH (port outward, starboard home) for the passengers. It may be this was before the word 'posh' became linked to the acronym story - posh was a word always associated with being smart in appearance.
22. C.Bailey, *Down the Burma Road*, Southampton (1990) p.56.
23. First Class stationery was thicker hand made paper, with the maker's watermark in it. All other writing paper was of an inferior quality, trimmed and with the White Star watermark.
24. The Audit House was wrongly identified in newspaper reports as the Guildhall (see *Titanic Voices*). At this time the Guildhall was in the Bargate and did not have pillars. The Audit House was the only municipal building with pillars. The present Guildhall, in the Civic Centre, was built in the 1930s.
25. See Appendix 2.
26. The women were not to know that Capt. Rostron gave the order not to pick up any bodies for fear of causing the survivors on board any more distress. Therefore, should anyone have been still alive, but unconscious in the water, they would have been left behind as a 'body'.
27. [illegible], the pilot who had guided *Titanic* down the Solent was George Bowyer, the Mayor's brother.
28. This was not discovered for many years until he required kidney surgery, much later in life. The pathology report recorded kidney scar tissue which was the result of damage received (possibly by a fall) while still an infant.
29. Eaton, J. and Haas, C. *Titanic – Triumph and Tragedy* Patrick Stephens Ltd, Yeovil (1995).p.207. It is worth noting that Ismay's wife served on the Liverpool Local Committee of the Titanic Fund. (Titanic Fund Regulations 1913)
30. B. Beed, *Titanic Victims in Halifax Graveyards* Dtours, Canada (2001) pp.45-6.
31. A. Patterson, (1971) p.96.
32. A. Rance, *Southampton, an illustrated history*, Southampton (1986) p.115; A. Patterson, (1971) pp.67, 75; J.L.B. James, *James Trevaskis – a study in personality*, Southampton (undated) pp.45-6.
33. St Luke's Parish Magazine May 1912.
34. Consumption was the general term used for pulmonary tuberculosis.
35. 'Game' was an expression for very brave actions. The critic was Sir Tommy Sopwith, who showed himself to be unaware of the expected roles of crewmen, especially stewards on liners. Possibly this was due to his own different experiences with the large sailing yachts. Two letters from correspondents, Wily and Mortimer, give the full details of the role of the stewards during a shipwreck. At all times their duty lay with the passengers, including ensuring that blankets were loaded into the lifeboats, and returning below to lock cabins 'to prevent pilfering.' (*Southern Daily Echo* 12 May 1912).
36. Leonard Hoare apparently gave his age as 16 when he signed on the *Titanic*. Many men lied about their ages, but usually it was the older men who gave younger ages, while younger individuals claimed to be older, to enrich their years of experience. Why Leonard did the opposite must remain a mystery, but his birth is recorded in Southampton during the Autumn of 1893 therefore, making him seventeen years old in April 1912. Perhaps he just forgot or was even unaware that he had had another birthday.
37. Winifred washed and ironed the waistcoat every year, until it was passed on to Teddy. The duty of annually washing the waistcoat, using traditional household soap, has now passed to the third generation.
38. H.R.O. COPY 816/D8; 226M86/LB3.
39. At this time the pound was made up of 240 pennies, so ten shillings was equivalent to 120 pennies, therefore small amounts of a few pennies would take a while to accumulate to the full amount, hence the weekly collection. If any of the boys received 'pocket money' from their families (possibly no more than three pence a week) it was likely they had to pay for the trip themselves, out of their pocket money.
40. Most theatres at this time gave two evening performances, referred to as the first and second houses.
41. The old Blighmont estate of fifty acres had stretched between Regent's Park Road and Waterhouse Lane, at the same time extending down to Millbrook Road. When the estate was split up the house remained to serve as a Nursing or Convalescent Home, together with part of the original walled garden and a few farm outbuildings; British American Tobacco bought a large section for its factory and sections were used for new roads and housing. It is likely that all three families were actually living within the bounds of the original estate at the start of the Second World War.

42. It appears that he has confused the date of sailing with the date he is probably writing the account. From newspaper reports of the storm and the evidence of his own discharge book, the date should be 4 February 1904.

43. Fred's spelling is phonetic and this is probably Savanña la Mer in Jamaica.

44. The 14th was a Sunday as stated in the text and so it appears that Fred was writing his account the following day while events were fresh in his mind.

45. 'Napper' is colloquial for head.

46. 'Chops' slang for mouth.

47. Fred seems to have made a slip with the date here. In 1894 he would have only been eight years old. It is more likely it should be 1904 as he signed off the *Clyde* on 6 August and didn't go back to sea until 23 September when he signed on with the *Magdalena* as a waiter. This would have given him sufficient time for the ride and account for the delay before he went back to sea, due to his recovery time.

48. 'Sit up' is another colloquialism, referring to anything which comes as a shock, usually in the form of sudden pain.

Selected Bibliography

Manuscript Sources

Private Collections

James Family Archive

Simmons Family Archive

Hampshire Archives & Local Studies

COPY 816/D8 Receipt for donation to Titanic Fund

226M86/LB3 School donation to Titanic Fund

Southampton Local History Library

Census returns for Southampton 1881, 1891, 1911.

Southampton Record Office

D/WW 1/1 Titanic Fund Second Minute Book

N.B. There are a few loose pages which have the same reference and some page numbers are duplicated. (These could be from the lost First Minute Book).

Ac 5297 1082/E 1913 Titanic Fund Schedule for money distribution – photocopy of printed schedule.

G23/123/21, 1912-13, Titanic Fund correspondence

G23/199/3, 1979-93, Titanic Fund correspondence

Merchant Seaman Identity Cards – Titanic survivors only. Copies kept separately with Titanic reference materials.

SC/EN 4/1/22A Eastern Board School Architect drawings

SC/E 6/12/2-5 Eastern Board School Log

SC/E 6/24/6-9 Northam School Log

SC/E 6/14/3 Freemantle School Log

PR20/1/6 St Luke's Baptism Register

PR 20/8/29 St Luke's Parish Magazine May 1912

PR 20/12/5-6;/17;/24a St Luke's images

PR 10/1/22; PR 10/1/14-15 Holy Trinity Parish Registers (Millbrook)

P149/1/131 Blighmont Nursing Home 1941

98131/1902; 98131/1904 RMSP Clyde crew lists

Transcript of oral history interview with Ernest Edmonds

The National Archives

BT/100/259 Titanic crew lists and other correspondence (microfiche)

BT 334/53 Board of Trade record of Seamen's Deaths

Printed Sources

Bailey, C., *Down the Burma Road*, Southampton (1990)

Beed, B. *Titanic Victims in Halifax Graveyards* Dtours, Canada (2001)

Douch, R., Visitors' Descriptions Southampton 1540-1956 *Southampton Papers No.2* Southampton (1978).

Doughty, M., *Dilapidated Housing and Housing Policy in Southampton 1890 – 1914* Southampton Records Series Vol 29 Southampton. (1986).

Eaton, J. and Haas, C. *Titanic – Triumph and Tragedy* Patrick Stephens Ltd, Yeovil (1995).

Encyclopaedia Titanica website

Hampshire Chronicle

Hyslop, D., Forsyth, A. and Jemima, S. *Titanic Voices* Southampton City Council, Huddersfield (1994).

James, J.L.B., *James Trevaskis – a study in personality*, Southampton (undated).

Le Faye, D., *Jane Austen's Letters* Oxford, (1997).

Lightholler, C., *Titanic and Other Ships*, Bay Tree Books No 1, Manchester (undated).

Lord, W., *A Night to Remember* London (1956).

Patterson, A., *A History of Southampton, Vol II The Beginnings of Modern Southampton*, Southampton Record Series, Southampton (1971).

Patterson, A., *A History of Southampton, Vol III Setbacks and Recoveries 1868-1914*, Southampton Record Series, Southampton (1975).

Southern Evening Echo.

Street Directories for Southampton - various years.